180 Days of SOCIAL STUDIES for Sixth Grade

Authors

Kathy Flynn, M.Ed., Terri McNamara, M.Ed., Marla Tomlinson

SHELL EDUCATION

Publishing Credits

Corinne Burton, M.A.Ed., *Publisher*
Conni Medina, M.A.Ed., *Managing Editor*
Emily R. Smith, M.A.Ed., *Content Director*
Veronique Bos, *Creative Director*

Developed and Produced by
Focus Strategic Communications, Inc.

Project Manager: Adrianna Edwards
Editor: Ron Edwards, Linda Jenkins
Designer and Compositor: Tracy Westell
Proofreader: Audrey Dorsch
Photo Researcher: Paula Joiner
Art: Tracy Westell

Image Credits:

p.29 National Park Maps; p.30 Library of Congress [LC-USF346-024776-D]; p.41 GL Archive/Alamy; p.44 (right) Paul Fearn/Alamy; p.50 Riksarkivet (National Archives of Norway)/NBR0214_00107; p.53 SOTK2011/Alamy; p.52 Botsford, George Willis. A History of Greece for High Schools and Academies. New York: Macmillan Co.; p.53 (bottom left) Godot13/Smithsonian Institution [Public domain] via Wikimedia Commons; p.53 (right) By PHGCOM (Own work, photographed at Tokyo Currency Museum), via Wikimedia Commons; p.62 (top left) Everett Historical/Shutterstock; p.62 (top right) Georgios Kollidas/Shutterstock; p.62 (bottom) Maksym Deliyergiyev/Shutterstock; p.64 Blulz60/Shutterstock; p.65 Library of Congress Geography and Map Division; p.66 Rosenau, M. J., Whipple, George Chandler, Trask, John W. and Salmon, Thomas William. Preventive Medicine and Hygiene. New York, London, D. Appleton. 1917; p.67 By Ali Zifan, via Wikimedia Commons; p.68 (top, bottom) NOAA/National Centers for Environmental Information; p.80 Evgenii Sribnyi/Shutterstock; p.81 meunierd/Shutterstock; p.82 ID1974/Shutterstock; p.84 (right) Sputnik/Alamy; p.85 Library of Congress [LC-DIG-ppmsca-08370]; p.90 (left) emkaplin/Shutterstock; p.90 (center) Hung Chung Chih/Shutterstock; p.90 (right) Library of Congress [LC-USZ62-101877]; p.92 (top) By Smurfy (Own work) [Public domain], via Wikimedia Commons; p.92 (bottom) By Ichwan Palongeng, via Wikimedia Commons; p.95 (center) Heritage Image Partnership Ltd/Alamy; p.95 (right), p.97 World History Archive/Alamy; p.96 (left) suronin/Shutterstock; p.96 (right) Mike Goldwater/Alamy; p.99 (left) Science History Images/Alamy; p.99 (right) robertharding/Alamy; p.100 360b/Shutterstock; p.104 (center) hanohiki/Shutterstock; p.105 Library of Congress Geography and Map Division; p.106 Library of Congress, Geography and Map Division; p.108 Romary/Wikimedia Commons; p.109 (top) By Demis BV [Public domain], via Wikimedia Commons; p.109 (bottom) erind/vecteezy.com; p.110 Therina Groenewald/Shutterstock; p.116 DnDavis/Shutterstock; p.121 Library of Congress [LC-DIG-pga-11392]; p.123 (bottom) A. Katz/Shutterstock; p.124 (right) Joseph Sohm/Shutterstock; p.129 Interfoto/Alamy; p.130 (top) Library of Congress [HAER IND,21-CONVI,3—1]; p.135 GL Archive/Alamy; p.143 (left) iStock.com/simongurney; p.143 (right) GlobalTravelPro/Shutterstock; p.145 U.S. Energy Information Administration; p.146 Fotos593/Shutterstock; p.150 NOAA/National Weather Service; p.154 (bottom) Katherine Welles/Shutterstock; p.161, p.164 (top) Frederic Legrand-Comeo/Shutterstock; p.162, p.164 (center), p.184 (center) Kathy Hutchins/Shutterstock; p.163, p.164 (bottom) JStone/Shutterstock; p.177 Chronicle/Alamy; p.182 Terri Brentnall/Alamy; p.183 Library of Congress [LC-DIG-ppmsca-47006]; p.184 (top) ale-kup/Shutterstock; p.184 (bottom) Library of Congress [LC-DIG-ppmsca-47006]; all other images from iStock and/or Shutterstock.

Standards

© 2014 Mid-continent Research for Education and Learning (McREL)
© 2010 National Council for the Social Studies (NCSS), The College, Career, and Civic Life (C3) Framework for Social Studies State Standards: Guidance for Enhancing the Rigor of K–12 Civics, Economics, Geography, and History

For information on how this resource meets national and other state standards, see pages 12–14. You may also review this information by visiting our website at www.teachercreatedmaterials.com/administrators/correlations/ and following the on-screen directions.

Shell Education

A division of Teacher Created Materials
5301 Oceanus Drive
Huntington Beach, CA 92649-1030
www.tcmpub.com/shell-education

ISBN 978-1-4258-1398-7
©2018 Shell Educational Publishing, Inc.

Table of Contents

Introduction

In the complex global world of the 21st century, it is essential for citizens to have the foundational knowledge and analytic skills to understand the barrage of information surrounding them. An effective social studies program will provide students with these analytic skills and prepare them to understand and make intentional decisions about their country and the world. A well-designed social studies program develops active citizens who are able to consider multiple viewpoints and the possible consequences of various decisions.

The four disciplines of social studies enable students to understand their relationships with other people—those who are similar and those from diverse backgrounds. Students come to appreciate the foundations of the American democratic system and the importance of civic involvement. They have opportunities to understand the historic and economic forces that have resulted in the world and United States of today. They will also explore geography to better understand the nature of Earth and the effects of human interactions.

It is essential that social studies addresses more than basic knowledge. In each grade, content knowledge is a vehicle for students to engage in deep, rich thinking. They must problem solve, make decisions, work cooperatively as well as alone, make connections, and make reasoned value judgments. The world and the United States are rapidly changing. Students must be prepared for the world they will soon lead.

The Need for Practice

To be successful in today's social studies classrooms, students must understand both basic knowledge and the application of ideas to new or novel situations. They must be able to discuss and apply their ideas in coherent and rational ways. Practice is essential if they are to internalize social studies concepts, skills, and big ideas. Practice is crucial to help students have the experience and confidence to apply the critical-thinking skills needed to be active citizens in a global society.

Introduction *(cont.)*

Understanding Assessment

In addition to providing opportunities for frequent practice, teachers must be able to assess students' understanding of social studies concepts, big ideas, vocabulary, and reasoning. This is important so teachers can effectively address students' misconceptions and gaps, build on their current understanding, and challenge their thinking at an appropriate level. Assessment is a long-term process that involves careful analysis of student responses from a multitude of sources. In the social studies context, this could include classroom discussions, projects, presentations, practice sheets, or tests. When analyzing the data, it is important for teachers to reflect on how their teaching practices may have influenced students' responses and to identify those areas where additional instruction may be required. Essentially, the data gathered from assessment should be used to inform instruction: to slow down, to continue as planned, to speed up, or to reteach in a new way.

Best Practices for This Series

- Use the practice pages to introduce important social studies topics to your students.

- Use the Weekly Topics and Themes chart from pages 5–7 to align the content to what you're covering in class. Then, treat the pages in this book as jumping off points for that content.

- Use the practice pages as formative assessment of the key social studies disciplines: history, civics, geography, and economics.

- Use the weekly themes to engage students in content that is new to them.

- Encourage students to independently learn more about the topics introduced in this series.

- Challenge students with some of the more complex weeks by leading teacher-directed discussions of the vocabulary and concepts presented.

- Support students in practicing the varied types of questions asked throughout the practice pages.

- Use the texts in this book to extend your teaching of close reading, responding to text-dependent questions, and providing evidence for answers.

How to Use This Book

180 Days of Social Studies offers teachers and parents a full page of social studies practice for each day of the school year.

Weekly Structure

These activities reinforce grade-level skills across a variety of social studies concepts. The content and questions are provided as full practice pages, making them easy to prepare and implement as part of a classroom routine or for homework.

Every practice page provides content, questions, and/or tasks that are tied to a social studies topic and standard. Students are given opportunities for regular practice in social studies, allowing them to build confidence through these quick standards-based activities.

Weekly Topics and Themes

The activities are organized by a weekly topic within one of the four social studies disciplines: history, civics, geography, and economics. The following chart shows the topics that are covered during each week of instruction:

Week	Discipline	Social Studies Topic	C3 Theme
1	History	Paleolithic era to agricultural revolution	Culture; People, places, and environments
2	Civics	The origins and purposes of government—Ancient Greece	Civic ideals and practices; Culture
3	Geography	Using maps and other tools to report information	People, places, and environments
4	Economics	Development of agriculture and the creation of economic surplus	Production, distribution, and consumption
5	History	Early Civilizations—Mesopotamia, Egypt	Time, continuity, and change
6	Civics	The origins and purposes of government—Ancient Rome	Civic ideals and practices; Culture
7	Geography	Mapping—Locating and comparing locations (including latitude and longitude)	People, places, and environments
8	Economics	Traditional economic systems and trade	Production, distribution, and consumption; People, places, and environments
9	History	Ancient Civilizations—Kush and the Ancient Hebrews	People, places, and environments; Culture

How to Use This Book (cont.)

Week	Discipline	Social Studies Topic	C3 Theme
10	Civics	Limited and unlimited government	Civic ideals and practices; Power, authority, and governance
11	Geography	Thematic geographic tools	People, places, and environments
12	Economics	Market economies	Production, distribution, and consumption
13	History	Ancient Greece	Time, continuity, and change; Civic ideals and practices
14	Civics	Compare and contrast modern governments, e.g., China, Germany, India, Russia	Civic ideals and practices; Power, authority, and governance
15	Geography	Relationship between ecosystems/physical features and populations	People, places, and environments
16	Economics	Command economies	Production, distribution, and consumption; Global connections
17	History	Ancient India	Time, continuity, and change; Individuals, groups, and institutions
18	Civics	Compare and contrast modern governments, e.g., China, Germany, India, Russia	Civic ideals and practices; Power, authority, and governance
19	Geography	Geographic patterns that result from the physical environment	People, places, and environment
20	Economics	Mixed economic systems	Production, distribution, and consumption
21	History	Ancient China	Time, continuity, and change; Power, authority, and governance
22	Civics	Roles, rights, and responsibilities of citizens—United States	Power, authority, and governance; Civic ideals and practices
23	Geography	Thematic tools—Ancient civilizations	People, places, and environment

51398—180 Days of Social Studies

© *Shell Education*

How to Use This Book (cont.)

Week	Discipline	Social Studies Topic	C3 Theme
24	Economics	Factors influencing production	Production, distribution, and consumption
25	History	Ancient Rome	Time, continuity, and change; Civic ideals and practices
26	Civics	Roles, rights, and responsibilities of citizens—Other countries	Civic ideals and practices; Individuals, groups, and institutions
27	Geography	Human impacts on the environment	People, places, and environments
28	Economics	Scarcity and decision-making	Production, distribution, and consumption
29	History	Mesoamerican Civilizations	Time, continuity, and change
30	Civics	Civic participation—In various countries	Civic ideals and practices; Power, authority, and governance
31	Geography	Characteristics and distribution of the migration of humans	People, places, and environments
32	Economics	Categories of economic activity and the national economy	Production, distribution, and consumption
33	History	Conflict, colonization, immigration, and trade	Time, continuity, and change; People, places, and environments
34	Civics	Opportunities for civic participation	Civic ideals and practices
35	Geography	Interpreting past and present patterns and planning for the future	People, places, and environments; Global connections
36	Economics	The United States and international trade	Production, distribution, and consumption; Global connections

How to Use This Book (cont.)

Using the Practice Pages

Practice pages provide instruction and assessment opportunities for each day of the school year. Days 1 to 4 provide content in short texts or graphics followed by related questions or tasks. Day 5 provides an application task based on the week's work.

All four social studies disciplines are practiced. There are nine weeks of topics for each discipline. The discipline is indicated on the margin of each page.

Day 1: Students read a text about the weekly topic and answer questions. This day provides a general introduction to the week's topic.

Day 2: Students read a text and answer questions. Typically, this content is more specialized than Day 1.

Day 3: Students analyze a primary source or other graphic (chart, table, graph, or infographic) related to the weekly topic and answer questions.

How to Use This Book *(cont.)*

Using the Practice Pages *(cont.)*

Day 4: Students analyze an image or text and answer questions. Then, students make connections to their own lives.

Day 5: Students analyze a primary source or other graphic and respond to it using knowledge they've gained throughout the week. This day serves as an application of what they've learned.

Diagnostic Assessment

Teachers can use the practice pages as diagnostic assessments. The data analysis tools included with the book enable teachers or parents to quickly score students' work and monitor their progress. Teachers and parents can see which skills students may need to target further to develop proficiency.

Students will learn skills to support informational text analysis, primary source analysis, how to make connections to self, and how to apply what they learned. To assess students' learning in these areas, check their answers based on the answer key or use the *Response Rubric* (page 212) for constructed-response questions that you want to evaluate more deeply. Then, record student scores on the *Practice Page Item Analysis* (page 213). You may also wish to complete a *Student Item Analysis by Discipline* for each student (pages 214–215). These charts are also provided in the Digital Resources as PDFs, *Microsoft Word®* files, and *Microsoft Excel®* files. Teachers can input data into the electronic files directly on the computer, or they can print the pages. See page 216 for more information.

How to Use This Book *(cont.)*

Diagnostic Assessment *(cont.)*

Practice Page Item Analyses

Every four weeks, follow these steps:

- Choose the four-week range you're assessing in the first row.

- Write or type the students' names in the far left column. Depending on the number of students, more than one copy of the form may be needed.

  - The skills are indicated across the top of the chart.

- For each student, record how many correct answers they gave and/or their rubric scores in the appropriate columns. There will be four numbers in each cell, one for each week. You can view which students are or are not understanding the social studies concepts or student progress after multiple opportunities to respond to specific text types or question forms.

- Review students' work for the first four sections. Add the scores for each student, and write that sum in the far right column. Use these scores as benchmarks to determine how each student is performing.

Student Item Analyses by Discipline

For each discipline, follow these steps:

- Write or type the student's name on the top of the charts.

  - The skills are indicated across the tops of the charts.

- Select the appropriate discipline and week.

- For each student, record how many correct answers they gave and/or their rubric scores in the appropriate columns. You can view which students are or are not understanding each social studies discipline or student progress after multiple opportunities to respond to specific text types or question forms.

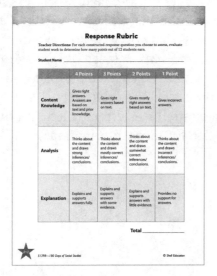

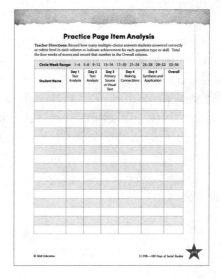

How to Use This Book *(cont.)*

Using the Results to Differentiate Instruction

Once results are gathered and analyzed, teachers can use the results to inform the way they differentiate instruction. The data can help determine which social studies skills and content are the most difficult for students and which students need additional instructional support and continued practice. Depending on how often the practice pages are scored, results can be considered for instructional support on a weekly or monthly basis.

Whole-Class Support

The results of the diagnostic analysis may show that the entire class is struggling with a particular concept or group of concepts. If these concepts have been taught in the past, this indicates that further instruction or reteaching is necessary. If these concepts have not been taught in the past, this data is a great preassessment and demonstrate that students do not have a working knowledge of the concepts. Thus, careful planning for the length of the unit(s) or lesson(s) must be considered, and extra front-loading may be required.

Small-Group or Individual Support

The results of the diagnostic analysis may show that an individual or a small group of students is struggling with a particular concept or group of concepts. If these concepts have been taught in the past, this indicates that further instruction or reteaching is necessary. Consider pulling aside these students while others are working independently to instruct further on the concept(s). You can also use the result to help identify individuals or groups of proficient students who are ready for enrichment or above-grade-level instruction. These students may benefit from independent learning contracts or more challenging activities.

Digital Resources

The Digital Resources contain PDFs and editable digital copies of the rubrics and item analysis pages. See page 216 for more information.

Standards Correlations

Shell Education is committed to producing educational materials that are research and standards based. In this effort, we have correlated all products to the academic standards of all 50 states, the District of Columbia, the Department of Defense Dependent Schools, and the Canadian provinces.

How to Find Standards Correlations

To print a customized correlation report of this product for your state, visit our website at **www.teachercreatedmaterials.com/administrators/correlations/** and follow the online directions. If you require assistance in printing correlation reports, please contact the Customer Service Department at 1-877-777-3450.

Purpose and Intent of Standards

The Every Student Succeeds Act (ESSA) mandates that all states adopt challenging academic standards that help students meet the goal of college and career readiness. While many states already adopted academic standards prior to ESSA, the act continues to hold states accountable for detailed and comprehensive standards.

Standards are designed to focus instruction and guide adoption of curricula. Standards are statements that describe the criteria necessary for students to meet specific academic goals. They define the knowledge, skills, and content students should acquire at each level. Standards are also used to develop standardized tests to evaluate students' academic progress. Teachers are required to demonstrate how their lessons meet state standards. State standards are used in the development of all of our products, so educators can be assured they meet the academic requirements of each state.

NCSS Standards and the C3 Framework

The lessons in this book are aligned to the National Council for the Social Studies (NCSS) standards and the C3 Framework. The chart on pages 5–7 lists the NCSS themes used throughout this book.

McREL Compendium

Each year, McREL analyzes state standards and revises the compendium to produce a general compilation of national standards. The chart on pages 13–14 correlates specific McREL standards to the content covered each week.

Standards Correlations *(cont.)*

Week	McREL Standard
1	Understands family life now and in the past, and family life in various places long ago.
2	Understands the sources, purposes, and functions of law, and the importance of the rule of law for the protection of individual rights and the common good.
3	Understands the characteristics and uses of maps, globes, and other geographic tools and technologies.
4	Understands basic features of market structures and exchanges.
5	Understands how democratic values came to be, and how they have been exemplified by people, events, and symbols.
6	Understands ideas about civic life, politics, and government.
7	Knows the location of places, geographic features, and patterns of the environment.
8	Understands basic features of market structures and exchanges.
9	Understands how democratic values came to be, and how they have been exemplified by people, events, and symbols.
10	Understands ideas about civic life, politics, and government.
11	Knows the location of places, geographic features, and patterns of the environment.
12	Understands basic features of market structures and exchanges.
13	Understands how democratic values came to be, and how they have been exemplified by people, events, and symbols.
14	Understands the sources, purposes, and functions of law, and the importance of the rule of law for the protection of individual rights and the common good.
15	Understands the physical and human characteristics of place Understands the nature and complexity of Earth's cultural mosaics.
16	Understands the roles government plays in the United States economy.
17	Understands family life now and in the past, and family life in various places long ago.
18	Understands ideas about civic life, politics, and government.
19	Understands the concept of regions Understands the physical and human characteristics of place.
20	Understands that scarcity of productive resources requires choices that generate opportunity costs.
21	Understands the folklore and other cultural contributions from various regions of the United States and how they helped to form a national heritage.

Standards Correlations *(cont.)*

Week	McREL Standard
22	Understands ideas about civic life, politics, and government.
23	Understands the physical and human characteristics of place. Understands the patterns of human settlement and their causes.
24	Understands that scarcity of productive resources requires choices that generate opportunity costs. Understands basic features of market structures and exchanges.
25	Understands the folklore and other cultural contributions from various regions of the United States and how they helped to form a national heritage.
26	Understands ideas about civic life, politics, and government.
27	Understands the physical and human characteristics of place. Understands how human actions modify the physical environment.
28	Understands that scarcity of productive resources requires choices that generate opportunity costs.
29	Understands major discoveries in science and technology, some of their social and economic effects, and the major scientists and inventors responsible for them.
30	Understands how certain character traits enhance citizens' ability to fulfill personal and civic responsibilities. Understands the roles of voluntarism and organized groups in American social and political life.
31	Understands the changes that occur in the meaning, use, distribution and importance of resources. Understands how human actions modify the physical environment.
32	Understands that scarcity of productive resources requires choices that generate opportunity costs.
33	Understands the history of a local community and how communities in North America varied long ago.
34	Understands how certain character traits enhance citizens' ability to fulfill personal and civic responsibilities.
35	Understands the characteristics and uses of spatial organization of Earth's surface. Understands the changes that occur in the meaning, use, distribution and importance of resources.
36	Understands that scarcity of productive resources requires choices that generate opportunity costs.

Name: _____ Date: _____

Directions: Read the text, and answer the questions.

Humans have been living on Earth for thousands of years. For most of that time, humans depended mainly on foods found in the wild. Hunting, trapping, and fishing were used to catch animals. Humans searched for plants to eat. They collected plants such as fruits, seeds, and nuts. They also gathered shellfish and insects.

People tended to live in family groups of a few dozen people. They traveled over large areas to find enough food to support their needs. As a result, large villages or towns were rare, because few areas had enough resources to support a large group of people.

1. Why did people live in small groups?
   a. They didn't want to get along with lots of other people.
   b. It was hard to find enough food in one area.
   c. They did not want to build a town.
   d. It was easier to celebrate together.

2. What would be necessary for hunter-gatherers to form a village?
   a. someone who wanted a town
   b. many families with lots of children
   c. houses that were made of the same material
   d. an area with a very rich supply of wild foods

3. Based on the text, what types of food did hunters and gathers search for?
   a. animals and shellfish
   b. plants and insects
   c. fruits, seeds, and nuts
   d. all the above

History

Name:_____ Date:_____

Directions: Read the text, and answer the questions.

Over 14,000 years ago, in the Paleolithic period, humans used tools. They used the tools to hunt animals. They used fire to cook and to preserve meat. Preserving food was a way to prepare for times when food was lacking.

Paleolithic humans made many kinds of stone tools. They made knives, scrapers, arrowheads, and axes. It is also likely that they used softer materials like ivory, bone, and wood. However, these tools made of softer materials have not survived to be examined today.

stone axe

1. Why was fire an important tool for Paleolithic humans?
   a. to signal for others
   b. to scare away animals
   c. to cook and preserve meat
   d. to tell the time of day

2. Look at the image. How can you tell that this stone axe was made by a human?
   a. There are marks where bits of stone were chipped off.
   b. It does not look very sharp.
   c. It looks like something found in nature.
   d. You can see tooth and claw marks.

3. What is one reason Paleolithic people may have made tools with ivory, bone, and wood?
   a. They wanted anyone to be able to make them.
   b. They did not want to waste materials they hunted or collected.
   c. They liked the texture and look of these materials.
   d. They were easier to carve than stone.

Name:_____ Date:_____

Directions: Look at the graphic, and answer the questions.

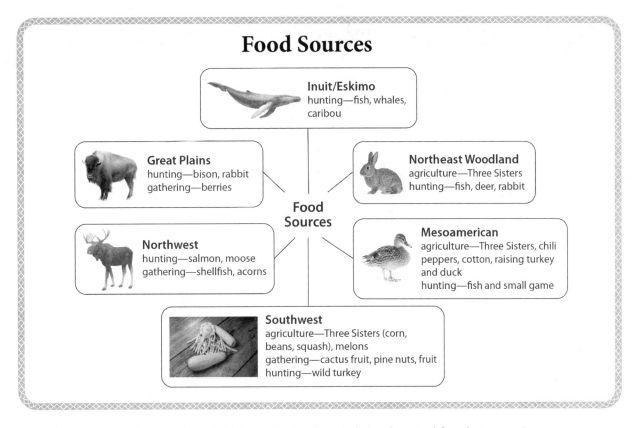

Food Sources

Inuit/Eskimo
hunting—fish, whales, caribou

Great Plains
hunting—bison, rabbit
gathering—berries

Northeast Woodland
agriculture—Three Sisters
hunting—fish, deer, rabbit

Food Sources

Northwest
hunting—salmon, moose
gathering—shellfish, acorns

Mesoamerican
agriculture—Three Sisters, chili peppers, cotton, raising turkey and duck
hunting—fish and small game

Southwest
agriculture—Three Sisters (corn, beans, squash), melons
gathering—cactus fruit, pine nuts, fruit
hunting—wild turkey

1. Why do you think the Inuit/Eskimo depend mainly on hunted food sources?

   a. They preferred the taste of food from the sea.

   b. Few edible plants grow in the cold Arctic.

   c. They liked hunting.

   d. The summers were very long.

2. How did raising animals help people get enough meat?

   a. People had the types of meat they liked.

   b. People didn't have to feed the animals.

   c. People did not have to hunt for the animals.

   d. The animals were bigger.

3. People in the Northwest built large communities, even though they did not grow a lot of food. What can you infer about the amount of food found in the wild in that region?

   _____

   _____

   _____

History

Name: _____ **Date:** _____

Directions: Read the chart, and answer the questions.

Types of Goods	
Society	**Goods**
hunter-gatherers—have to move from place to place to find food	simple tools portable shelter clothing
agricultural societies—can stay in one place for several or many years	permanent shelters pottery, cooking, and storage materials clothing stored food simple toys fields for planting domesticated animals
modern societies	permanent shelters cars clothing toys technology food from stores

1. Hunter-gatherers had only a few goods. Why was this important for them?

    a. They needed to be able to travel long distances.

    b. They preferred to hunt rather than to make things.

    c. They did not want to be robbed.

    d. There were no places to buy or trade for goods.

2. Why did agricultural societies have more goods?

    _____

    _____

    _____

    _____

3. What could you learn about the importance of goods from a hunter-gatherer?

    _____

    _____

    _____

    _____

Name: _____ **Date:** _____

Directions: Study the image, and complete the task.

Scientists have learned a lot about ancient peoples by looking at their paintings on the walls of caves.

1. Draw a "wall painting" that shows something important about your life.

2. Compare your life with the life of the person who created the cave painting above.

_____

_____

_____

_____

Civics

Name: _____ Date: _____

Directions: Read the text, and circle the best answer for each question.

The ancient Greeks were well known for developing new ideas. In ancient Greece, Athens was an important city. It was here that democracy was first created to govern the people. Democracy would become one of the most important influences on modern governments.

At that time, Greece was made up of city-states. These were city areas with surrounding land. Each one had its own government and ruler(s).

In these city-states, there were three main types of government:

- democracy: rule by the people
- monarchy: rule by a king or a tyrant
- oligarchy: rule by a small powerful group

1. Based on the text, why did Athens become important?
   a. It was where a monarchy first ruled.
   b. It was where government was first created.
   c. It was where city-states were first developed.
   d. It was where democracy was first developed.

2. What were city-states?
   a. They were large areas of land with many cities.
   b. They included one city with surrounding land governed by its own ruler(s).
   c. They included one large city area governed by many rulers.
   d. They were made up of cities with one government and ruler(s).

3. There were three types of government in city-states. What was one of these?
   a. democracy, where government was ruled by a small powerful group
   b. oligarchy, where government was ruled by the people
   c. democracy, where government was ruled by the people
   d. monarchy, where government was ruled by a small powerful group

51398—180 Days of Social Studies   © *Shell Education*

Name:_____ Date:_____

Directions: Read the text, and circle the best answer for each question.

In the year 507 BC, the ruler of Athens was named Cleisthenes. He invented a government system called *demokrata*. This meant "rule by the people." It was the first form of democracy.

In this system, the citizens voted on everything. Only men who had military training were considered to be citizens, and only citizens could vote.

There were officials to help manage the government. They were chosen by a lottery so that all people had an equal chance of winning. It did not matter if they were wealthy or not. Only a few jobs were held by leaders who were voted for, such as army generals.

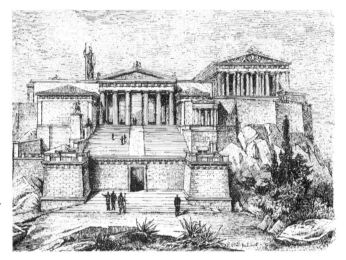

ancient Athens

1. What type of government was a *demokrata*?

   a. one where citizens voted for elected representatives in the government

   b. one that was ruled by the people, and citizens voted

   c. one that was ruled by a tyrant, and citizens did not vote

   d. one that was ruled by a king, and citizens did not vote

2. How were the citizens of ancient Athens different from the citizens of our country?

   a. Citizens of ancient Athens were all the adults, but not the children.

   b. Citizens of ancient Athens were all the adults and the children.

   c. Citizens of ancient Athens were all adult men with military training.

   d. Citizens of ancient Athens were men and women with military training.

3. How did government officials come into their jobs?

   a. They were elected by the citizens.

   b. They applied for their jobs.

   c. They paid with their wealth.

   d. They were selected by a lottery.

Civics

Name: _____ **Date:** _____

Directions: Look at the web, and answer the questions.

Facts about Democracy (*Demokrata*) in Ancient Athens

The government was made up of:

- the Assembly, or the citizens who could vote.
- the Council of 500, or the people who got their jobs by lottery. They stayed in their jobs for one year.
- the Courts, or the judges and juries.

Demokrata lasted for about 200 years in ancient Athens, but it would impact the future.

There were about 250,000 people living in ancient Athens. About 150,000 of them were enslaved. Only about 40,000 people were citizens who could vote.

Parthenon temple on the Acropolis in Athens

1. What groups made up the *demokrata*?

a. the executive, legislative, and judicial

b. the monarch, the Senate, and the House of Commons

c. the Senate, the House of Representatives, and the Supreme Court

d. the Assembly, the Council of 500, and the Courts

2. What proportion of all the people living in ancient Athens could vote?

a. All the people could vote on laws.

b. About one half of the people could vote on laws.

c. Only a small group of all people could vote on laws.

d. Most of the people could vote on laws.

3. Democracy lasted only about two centuries in ancient Athens, but it would influence later governments. Describe which Americans can vote in our system of government.

_____

_____

51398—180 Days of Social Studies

Name:_____ Date:_____

Directions: Read the chart, and answer the questions.

Evolution of Democracy					
Ancient Athens	Early to Mid-1600s—arrival of Colonists in America	Late 1600s	150 Years Later	The American Revolution	The Constitution
The government created a type of democracy. It would one day inspire Americans.	The first colonists in America came from England. It was governed by a monarchy.	John Locke wrote about the right to life, liberty, and property. He believed the people should have the right to rebel against their government if the government took the people's rights away.	The colonists were overtaxed, and their rights were not protected. They wanted a new government. They felt they had the experience to run their government separate from the king's rule.	The American people fought for independence. They won the right to separate from the monarchy of Britain. They wrote the Constitution and created a new government to allow more freedom for citizens.	The Constitution stands for freedom and democracy. It has lasted longer than any other document of its kind. It is based on the democracy of ancient places and the writings of people such as John Locke.

1. John Locke wrote about people's rights. Which of these did they include?

    a. the right to a fair and speedy trial

    b. the right to bear arms to protect oneself

    c. the rights to life and liberty

    d. the rights to education and travel

2. Why did the people of America fight in a revolution?

    _____

    _____

    _____

3. Other beliefs influenced the Constitution. What were they? Which of these were included in the Constitution?

    _____

    _____

    _____

Civics

Name: _____ **Date:** _____

Directions: Read the text. Then, tell what you know about two of the following topics.

> The first ideas that would lead to democracy began long ago. Over many years, different people added their thoughts to improve this system.

1. Early democracy in ancient Athens:

_____

_____

_____

_____

_____

Ancient Athens

2. Before democracy in the American colonies:

_____

_____

_____

_____

_____

King George III

3. Early ideas that had an impact on the Constitution:

_____

_____

_____

_____

_____

John Locke

24

Geography

Name: _____ Date: _____

Directions: Read the text, and answer the questions.

There are many tools that we can use when we study physical geography. There are simple tools such as paper, maps, and globes. There are also high-tech tools such as the global positioning system (GPS). All these tools show key details in different ways. What these tools have in common is that they show location, measure distance, and help give context to an area.

Location is shown by lines called latitude and longitude. These lines divide Earth into measurable blocks.

Distance is measured using a scale that represents an area on the ground. For example, one inch can show 10 miles.

An area can be shown through topography (hills, valleys, and plateaus), streets and landmarks, or addresses.

1. Based on the text, what do geographical tools have in common?
   a. They show location.
   b. They measure distance.
   c. They provide context to an area.
   d. all the above

2. How can a small map represent the distance between cities?
   a. Maps use estimates for distance.
   b. Maps use scales to measure distances.
   c. Distance isn't important on a map.
   d. Distance can't be measured.

3. What is one way to show areas on a map?
   a. latitude lines
   b. bodies of water
   c. topography
   d. measuring distances

Geography

Name: _____ **Date:** _____

Directions: Read the chart, and answer the questions.

Geography Tools	
	A map is a diagram showing a place. It shows the area in a simple way and includes a scale to show distance. Maps can show larger-scale settlement patterns or country sizes. Maps can also show detailed information such as street names and house locations.
	An atlas is a collection of maps. Atlases are often bound as a book, but they can also be in digital format.
	A globe is a spherical map of Earth. Because it is a sphere, it shows a more accurate view of the sizes, shapes, and locations of places than a map does. Because maps are flat, they may distort areas.
	GPS stands for Global Positioning System. These devices use the satellites orbiting Earth to find locations. They are often used in vehicles.
	GIS stands for Geographical Information System. GIS is a computer system. It is used to manage and understand geographic data. It uses data from many different kinds of sources to provide information.

1. Why is a globe a more accurate view of Earth than a map?

   a. Because it is spherical, the countries aren't distorted.

   b. Globes include more countries than a map can.

   c. Maps are actually more accurate than globes.

   d. Globes include more information than maps.

2. If you were planning a car road trip in the United States, which mapping tool would be the most useful? Circle all that apply.

   a. a map   **c.** an atlas

   b. a globe   **d.** GIS

3. What geographical tool would be the most helpful if you were lost in a forest?

   a. a globe   **c.** a GPS

   b. an atlas   **d.** a map

Name: _____   Date: _____

Directions: Study the map, and answer the questions.

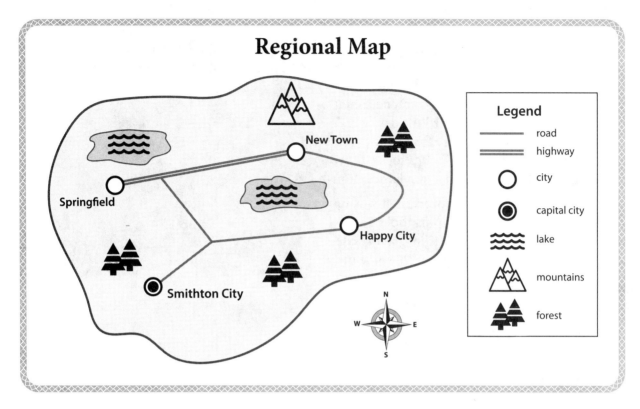

Geography

1. What city would you want to live in if you wanted to live near a lake and near the mountains?

   a. New Town

   b. Springfield

   c. Smithton City

   d. Happy City

2. Which of the following is true about New Town? Circle all that apply.

   a. It is connected to Smithton City by a highway.

   b. It is not near the mountains.

   c. It is directly next to the capital city.

   d. It is directly beside a lake.

3. Which natural features would you draw on a map about your region?

   _____

   _____

   _____

Name: _____ **Date:** _____

Directions: Read the text, and answer the questions.

Geography

Geocaching is a fun way for people to explore the world around them using geographic tools. It's like a real-life treasure hunt that starts online. A website provides the coordinates for you to find hidden containers called *caches*. Each cache contains a log book where you record the date you found it. You leave it there for the next person to find. They are hidden under rocks, in trees, in small holes, and in other similar locations.

People take part in geocaching by using a map, GPS, or other mapping tool or app. There are millions of geocaches around the world. In fact, there are probably some in your community.

1. How do people take part in geocaching?

    a. They have to buy the board game.

    b. They have to find a caching club.

    c. They go online to find the coordinates.

    d. They go to the library to find the start.

2. Where in your community would be a good place for you to hide your very own cache?

    _____

    _____

    _____

3. Have you ever taken part in geocaching? If so, what tools did you use and who did you go with? If not, what do you think you might use and who would you go geocaching with?

    _____

    _____

    _____

    _____

Name: ______________________________ **Date:** ______________

Directions: Look at the map, and draw your own map.

Harpers Ferry City Map

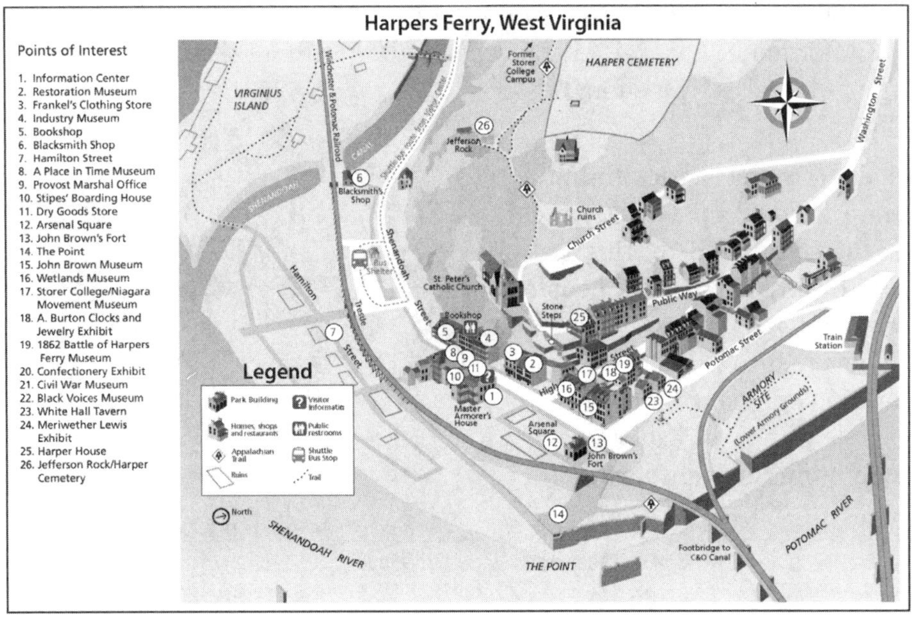

Harpers Ferry, West Virginia
Points of Interest
1. Information Center
2. Restoration Museum
3. Frankel's Clothing Store
4. Industry Museum
5. Bookshop
6. Blacksmith Shop
7. Hamilton Street
8. A Place in Time Museum
9. Provost Marshal Office
10. Stipes' Boarding House
11. Dry Goods Store
12. Arsenal Square
13. John Brown's Fort
14. The Point
15. John Brown Museum
16. Wetlands Museum
17. Storer College/Niagara Movement Museum
18. A. Burton Clocks and Jewelry Exhibit
19. 1862 Battle of Harpers Ferry Museum
20. Confectionery Exhibit
21. Civil War Museum
22. Black Voices Museum
23. White Hall Tavern
24. Meriwether Lewis Exhibit
25. Harper House
26. Jefferson Rock/Harper Cemetery
VIRGINIUS ISLAND
Winchester & Potomac Railroad
Blacksmith's Shop
Jefferson Rock
Former Storer College Campus
HARPER CEMETERY
Washington Street
Church ruins
Church Street
Shenandoah Street
Bus Shelter
St. Peter's Catholic Church
Hamilton
Trestle Street
Bookshop
Stone Steps
Public Way
Potomac Street
Train Station
High Street
Master Armorer's House
Arsenal Square
John Brown's Fort
ARMORY SITE
(Lower Armory Grounds)
Legend
Park Building
Visitor Information
Homes, shops and restaurants
Public restrooms
Appalachian Trail
Shuttle Bus Stop
Ruins
Trail
North
SHENANDOAH RIVER
THE POINT
Footbridge to C&O Canal
POTOMAC RIVER

1. Use the space below to draw a map of an imaginary city. Include buildings such as schools, fire stations, and a library. Also include some other points of interest. Use the Harpers Ferry map to get some ideas of what to include. Name your city. Draw a compass rose to show direction, and add a legend.

Economics

Name: _____ Date: _____

Directions: Read the text, and answer the questions.

For thousands of years, humans survived by hunting and gathering food. Gradually, they began to form more permanent communities. They learned to domesticate animals and use them for food. They raised crops. First, they were subsistence farmers. These were farmers who raised just enough for a family.

However, over time, agricultural methods improved. People could raise more food than they needed. This surplus could be traded to other people for different goods or services. Surplus allowed people to turn to activities beyond hunting or raising food. It also left people with new challenges—how to safely store and transport the surplus.

farming long ago

1. Based on the text, how did domesticated animals help humans?
   a. They ensured there would be meat available.
   b. They were pleasant to have around.
   c. They could be used for labor.
   d. They kept the children entertained.

2. Based on the text, what was the result of improving agricultural methods?
   a. People didn't need as many tools.
   b. People were able to harvest larger crops.
   c. People knew more about their world.
   d. People could have more variety.

3. What was a downfall of a surplus?
   a. People could trade for other goods or services.
   b. People could turn to other tasks.
   c. It led to methods of storing extra food.
   d. People had to figure out how to transport the surplus.

Name: _____ Date: _____

Directions: Read the text, and answer the questions.

Before civilizations could grow, people had to develop agriculture fully. This allowed farmers to grow surplus food. This meant they had to create new technology, including water control. Many early civilizations were located in river valleys that experienced flooding. At the same time, they were often in hot, dry places. This meant irrigation was important.

New engineering and building skills were needed. For example, the Mesopotamians designed a system to bring water where it was needed. People were also needed to build and repair the system. This was new work for people.

ancient water system in the Middle East

1. Why was water control necessary?

   a. to make sure there was water in the river

   b. to make sure dry fields had enough water

   c. to collect rain water

   d. to keep people dry during the rainy season

2. Why were engineers important?

   a. They drove the farm engines.

   b. They had jobs in the cities.

   c. They designed water systems.

   d. They kept the builders busy.

3. The government in the United States looks after large projects. These projects are important for the growth of the U.S. economy. Circle the project that helps many people in the United States.

   a. the interstate highway system

   b. someone's house

   c. a local church and parish hall

   d. a local school

Economics

Name: _____ **Date:** _____

Directions: Look at the images, and answer the questions.

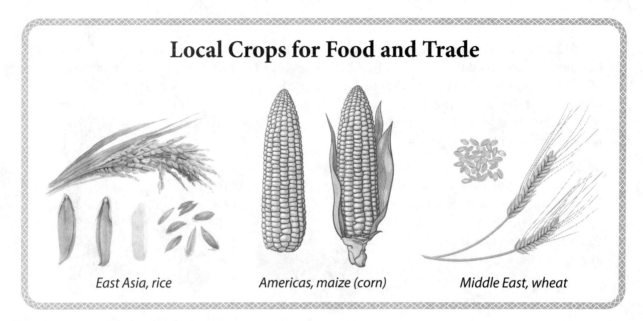

Local Crops for Food and Trade

East Asia, rice   *Americas, maize (corn)*   *Middle East, wheat*

1. Based on these images, what category of food did all these civilizations grow?
   a. fruit
   b. grain
   c. roots
   d. dairy

2. Why would these foods make good surplus foods?
   a. Children didn't like them.
   b. They kept for a long time.
   c. They rotted quickly.
   d. They were difficult to trade.

3. What might the farmers do with foods that didn't keep well?

   _____

   _____

   _____

   _____

   _____

Name: _____ **Date:** _____

Directions: Study the graphic, and answer the questions.

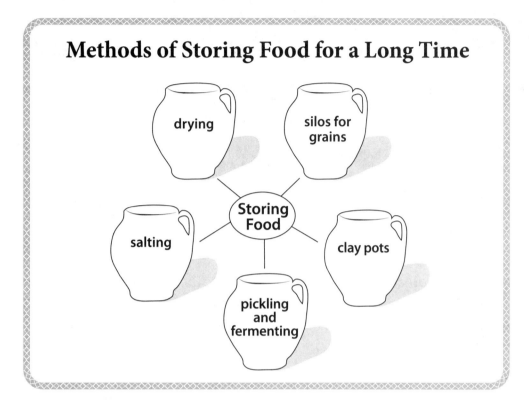

Methods of Storing Food for a Long Time

drying

silos for grains

Storing Food

salting

clay pots

pickling and fermenting

Economics

1. Why was food preservation important? Circle the two best answers.

   a. It saved food for times of famine or flood.

   b. They could trade food for other goods or services.

   c. They didn't want to throw it away.

   d. They liked to have many different choices available.

2. Think of the food in your home today. Which of these ancient methods of preserving have been used for those foods? Give an example for each one.

   _____

   _____

   _____

3. Describe two kinds of food preservation in your home that the ancient people did not use.

   _____

   _____

Name:_____ Date:_____

Economics

Directions: Look at the timeline, and answer the question.

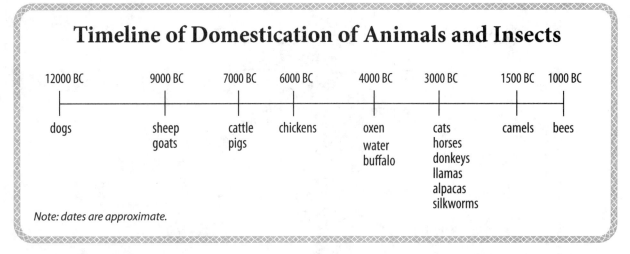

Timeline of Domestication of Animals and Insects

12000 BC	9000 BC	7000 BC	6000 BC	4000 BC	3000 BC	1500 BC	1000 BC
dogs	sheep goats	cattle pigs	chickens	oxen water buffalo	cats horses donkeys llamas alpacas silkworms	camels	bees

Note: dates are approximate.

1. Having domestic animals led to changes for humans. The animals were used for many things. How did these animals help humans long ago?

_____

_____

_____

_____

_____

_____

_____

_____

_____

_____

Name: _____ **Date:** _____

Directions: Read the text, and answer the questions.

About 10 to 15 thousand years ago, people began to grow plants for food and to tame animals. Planned agriculture meant that food became more available. People were able to stay in one place. They built larger communities than before. They needed clean water sources and fertile land. People built permanent houses. They could share duties and had more time for many other activities.

The people learned to use metals like bronze. They made better tools. Kingdoms, or states, were created. Leaders wrote laws to help people live together safely. Many early civilizations developed writing. They were able to write down business dealings and share their knowledge.

History

1. Why did people need agriculture before creating a large community?

   a. They were used to eating regular meals.

   b. They would get hungry and not have time to hunt.

   c. There would be enough wild food in the area to support a large population.

   d. It was important to make sure no one would starve in the new community.

2. Why was it important to develop laws?

   a. to make a job for police

   b. to make sure people were safe

   c. to make jobs for judges

   d. so that people knew what to do

3. Why did people form larger groups?

   a. People could share jobs and duties more efficiently.

   b. People wanted more contact with other people.

   c. More people were being born.

   d. Rulers wanted to be the boss of lots of people.

History

Name:_____ Date:_____

Directions: Read the text, and answer the questions.

Around 3100 BC, the Egyptians began to live in cities along the Nile River. The Nile River was key for the growth of this civilization. They used the river to transport goods and water their crops. The yearly flooding brought fresh soil to the fields.

A pharaoh led the society. The Egyptians created writing that could be used to share messages and information. They had many scientists and inventors who helped to build the huge pyramids. They invented the plow and papyrus (used like paper). They also made cosmetics and many herbal medicines. They were excellent shipbuilders.

1. Why were the banks of the Nile River a good place for a civilization to grow?
   a. The river was very small.
   b. The river was useful for recreation.
   c. The river had no wildlife.
   d. The river brought fertile soil when it flooded.

2. Based on the text, why was writing important for the Egyptian civilization?
   a. People could share messages and information.
   b. The pharaoh could keep track of what his people were doing.
   c. People could use their papyrus for cosmetics.
   d. The engineers could keep track of jobs for the workers.

3. The banks of the Nile were fertile areas. Why is it important for a group of people?

   _____

   _____

   _____

   _____

51398—180 Days of Social Studies

© *Shell Education*

Name: _____ **Date:** _____

Directions: Study the image, and answer the questions.

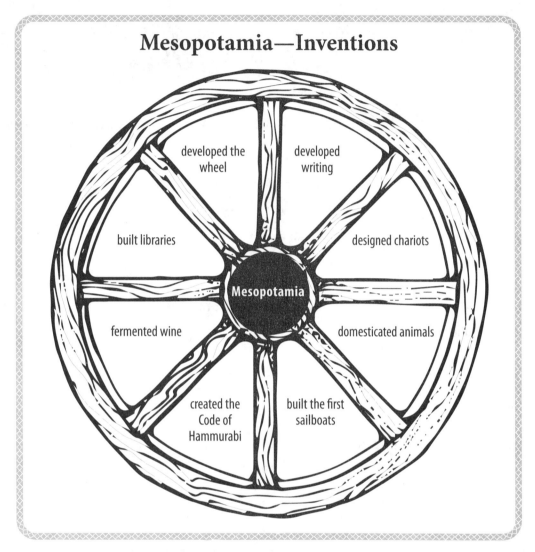

Mesopotamia—Inventions

developed the wheel

developed writing

built libraries

designed chariots

Mesopotamia

fermented wine

domesticated animals

created the Code of Hammurabi

built the first sailboats

1. Which advances were important for the Mesopotamians?

   a. developed writing, invented the wheel, fermented wine

   b. invented the wheel, developed writing, domesticated animals

   c. created the Code of Hammurabi, fermented wine, built sailboats

   d. all the above

2. Why was the invention of the wheel important for the Mesopotamians?

   a. It created new jobs for some people.

   b. It let them design different kinds of carts and wagons.

   c. They could move things more easily and quickly.

   d. It helped them domesticate animals.

History

Name:_____ Date:_____

Directions: Read the chart, and answer the questions.

The Code of Hammurabi	
Crime	**Punishment**
If you steal…	…you will be put to death.
If you don't take care of your dam and someone else's field is damaged…	…you will be sold as a slave and the money given to the other person.
If you damage someone's eye…	…your eye will be destroyed.
If you break someone's bone…	…your bone will be broken.
If a son hits his father…	…his hand will be cut off.
If a doctor kills a rich patient…	…his hands are cut off.
If the doctor kills a slave…	…he pays the owner.

1. According to the Code of Hammurabi, what is the punishment for damaging someone's eye?

   a. you are killed

   b. your eye is damaged

   c. your hand is cut off

   d. you are made a slave

2. Compare these laws to laws in the United States today.

   _____

   _____

   _____

   _____

3. Why do you think punishments today are different from those in Hammurabi's time?

   _____

   _____

   _____

   _____

51398—180 Days of Social Studies

Name:_____ Date:_____

Directions: Read the captions, and study the image. Complete the task.

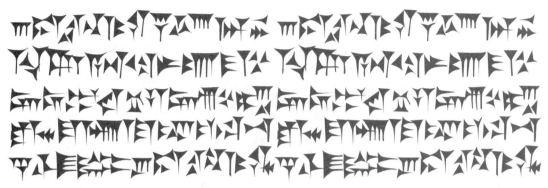

Sumerian cuneiform writing

Egyptian hieroglyphics

1. People developed writing when towns and cities formed. Why was writing important to the Mesopotamians and Egyptians?

    _____

    _____

    _____

    _____

    _____

    _____

    _____

Civics

Name: _____ Date: _____

Directions: Read the text, and circle the best answer for each question.

In 509 BC, the city of Rome was a republic, or place "of the people." Like ancient Athens, it was an early type of democracy. The government was run by laws and a constitution. The Romans wrote their laws on 12 bronze tablets that were displayed in the Roman Forum. The constitution was never written down. But it set up a system of checks and balances to make sure that no one person would have too much power.

Much of the government's power was held by two *consuls,* who were elected each year by the Roman people. The consuls also commanded the Roman army. Each one could veto the decisions made by the other. Furthermore, when they needed money, they had to ask for it from the Senate.

Roman Forum

1. What type of government do republics have?
   a. They have a monarchy where a king or queen rules.
   b. They have an oligarchy ruled by a small group of powerful people.
   c. They have a democratic government where the people vote.
   d. They have a government where only a president holds power.

2. Why are checks and balances an important part of a democratic system?
   a. They make sure that the king or queen has all the power.
   b. They give all the money to the most powerful people.
   c. They give all the power to just a small group of people.
   d. They limit the power of officials elected by the people.

3. What checks and balances kept each consul from being too powerful?
   a. Each consul had his own powerful group of supporters.
   b. Each consul had the right to veto and no direct access to money.
   c. Each consul had to ask the Assembly for everything before making a decision.
   d. Each consul could set taxes and laws when he wanted to.

Name:_____ **Date:**_____

Directions: Read the text, and look at the picture. Answer the questions.

In ancient Rome, the government was run by elected officials. Other than the consuls, there were the following:

Senate: They gave advice to the consuls and influenced their decisions. They were chosen from the wealthy class and held their jobs for the rest of their lives.

Plebeian Council: It was an assembly of people who voted for laws and elected their leaders.

Tribunes: They represented the poor people and gave them a say in government decisions.

Governors: The Roman armies defeated armies from other places and took over their lands. Then, they appointed governors to run the new governments and collect taxes from the people. The people became Roman citizens.

ancient Rome—the Senate

Civics

1. Why was the Senate powerful? Circle the two best answers.
   a. Senators were elected for life.
   b. Senators voted for laws.
   c. Senators represented all the poor people.
   d. Senators advised the consuls.

2. Based on the text, what did the governors do?
   a. participated in the Tribunes
   b. collected taxes from the people
   c. represented the poor people
   d. gave advice to the consuls

3. What would the Romans do after they conquered lands in other places?
   a. They set up governments with Plebeian Councils.
   b. They had governors govern the new citizens.
   c. They would win the battles, take the treasures, and leave.
   d. They set up consuls and Senates in the conquered lands.

Civics

Name:_____ Date:_____

Directions: Look at the web, and answer the questions.

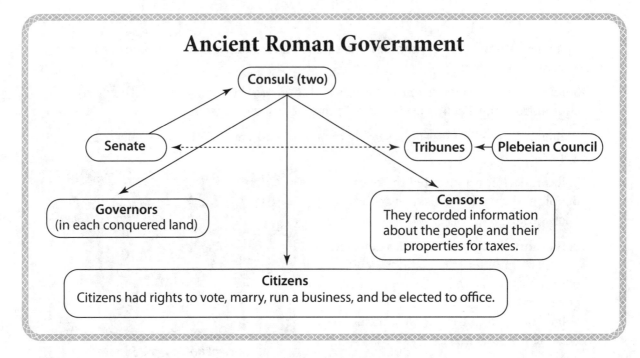

1. Each government role had power and responsibilities. Who had control over the citizens?

   a. Senate

   b. Consuls

   c. Censors

   d. Governors

2. What are some of the rights of Roman citizens?

   _____

   _____

   _____

3. If you were a government official in ancient Rome, which role would you prefer? Explain why.

   _____

   _____

   _____

   _____

Name: _____ Date: _____

Directions: Read the text, and answer the questions.

The ancient Greeks developed the first ideas about democracy. The ancient Romans had their own, different ideas. The U.S. government took some of its ideas from the ancient people but added its own, too.

Some people believe that government should protect people's freedoms. It should defend people's rights, and promote the common good. Some people believe that the government should help people with money. It should provide welfare and other social funds. It should make it easier to start businesses. And some people think that the government should supervise the choices people make about their religion.

Not everyone agrees on what *democracy* should mean. But we all want healthy lives, where we can feel safe and make choices for ourselves. If we did not have government, we would not have our rights, laws, community workers, and armed forces.

Roman Senator

1. Which of these does the U.S. government provide for its citizens?

   a. free computers, cellphones, and video games

   b. freedoms such as speaking and writing what we think

   c. protection from illness and disease

   d. free medicine, food, housing, and cars

2. Why is it a good idea for government to provide some services for poor, disabled, and senior people?

   _____

   _____

   _____

3. Should a democratic government tell people what religion to follow? Why or why not?

   _____

   _____

   _____

Civics

Name:_____ Date:_____

Directions: Democracy has changed since ancient Roman times. Over the years, many ideas about democracy have developed. Think about how the ancient Roman citizens were governed. How are we governed in our country today? Compare and contrast these two systems.

American Bill of Rights

ancient Roman Laws of Twelve Tables

_____

_____

_____

_____

_____

_____

_____

_____

_____

_____

_____

51398—180 Days of Social Studies

Name:_____ Date:_____

Directions: Read the text, and answer the questions.

Geography

Maps, GPSs, and other geographical tools help people to locate places. Maps have tools to help you find a location. Distance on a map is measured using a scale that represents length on the ground. Symbols are used to identify specific places. They also identify roads, bridges, and other structures. Grids are lines that cross each other to block out areas.

An example of a grid is latitude and longitude. Latitude and longitude are imaginary lines used to describe where a place is on Earth. Latitude lines are parallel to the equator. Longitude lines are parallel to the prime meridian. These lines show the exact coordinates.

1. How is distance measured on a map?

    a. A scale represents the actual distance.

    b. Latitude and longitude mark locations.

    c. Distance is marked by symbols and icons.

    d. Distance always goes in 10 degree blocks.

2. What do grids do?

    a. They show distance.

    b. They run east to west.

    c. They show icons of structures.

    d. They provide exact coordinates.

3. If you were looking for a specific school on a map, what is something you could look for?

    a. a grid section

    b. the prime meridian

    c. coordinates that relate to that school

    d. bridges near the school

Name: _____ **Date:** _____

Geography

Directions: Read the text, and look at the graphic. Answer the questions.

The equator runs around the middle of Earth. It is at 0° latitude. It divides Earth into Northern and Southern Hemispheres. The prime meridian is at 0° longitude. It divides Earth into the Eastern and Western hemispheres.

Everything north of the Arctic Circle is the Arctic. Everything south of the Antarctic Circle is the Antarctic.

The Tropic of Cancer is at the latitude of 23.5°N. The Tropic of Capricorn is at the latitude of 23.5°S.

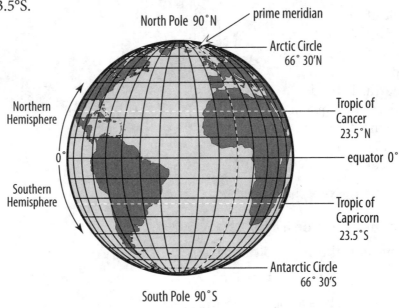

1. What is the line of latitude around the middle of Earth?

   a. the prime meridian   **c.** the Arctic Circle

   b. the Tropic of Cancer   **d.** the equator

2. Where is the Tropic of Capricorn located?

   a. the Southern Hemisphere

   b. the Eastern Hemisphere

   c. the Northern Hemisphere

   d. the Western Hemisphere

3. The Tropic of Cancer is at 23.5°N. Where is it located on Earth?

   a. east of the prime meridian

   b. north of the equator

   c. near the Antarctic Circle

   d. south of the equator

51398—180 Days of Social Studies

Name: _____ Date: _____

Directions: Study the map, and answer the questions.

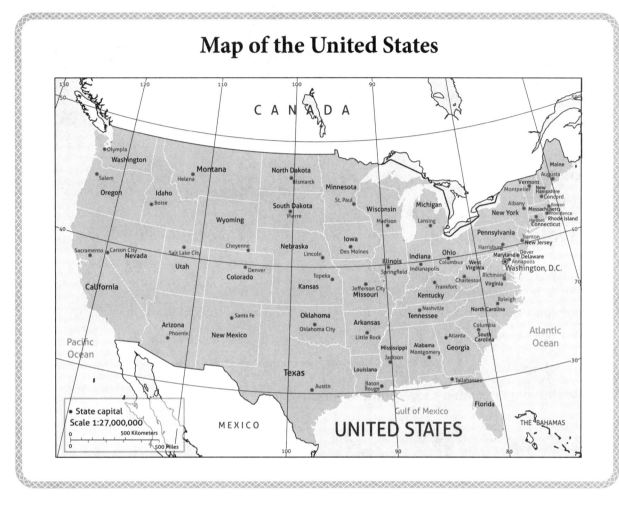

Map of the United States

1. What state capital is at 45° N and 93° W?

   a. Austin, TX

   b. Helena, MT

   c. Sacramento, CA

   d. St. Paul, MN

2. In what state would you find the coordinates 39° N and 98° W?

   a. Nevada

   b. Maine

   c. Kansas

   d. North Dakota

3. What are the approximate latitude and longitude of your community? What are the latitude and longitude of a capital city you would like to visit?

   _____

   _____

   _____

Geography

Name: _____ **Date:** _____

Directions: Read the text, and answer the questions.

Early cartographers used instruments such as a compass and telescope, and they used math equations. They even used the stars to guide them. Now mapmakers use computers, satellites, and other technological tools.

Not all maps show the same information. Some, such as city maps, are used to find directions. Other maps show the shape of Earth, such as hills and valleys. These are called topographical maps. Thematic maps look at specific types of information, such as the populations of certain areas or local temperatures..

1. What kind of map would show temperatures in different states?

   a. a city map

   b. a star map

   c. a thematic map

   d. a topographical map

2. How does technology help cartographers?

   _____

   _____

   _____

3. If you were a cartographer, what would you want to map: an urban or a rural area? Why?

   _____

   _____

   _____

Name: _____ Date: _____

Directions: Look at the images, and fill in the chart.

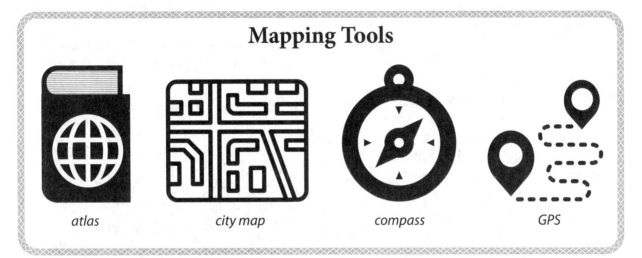

Mapping Tools

atlas   *city map*   *compass*   *GPS*

1. Think about the mapping tools above. Below is a series of places you might be. Which mapping tool would you use in each situation? Explain your answer.

shopping downtown	
traveling around the world	
camping	
driving to a different city	

Name:_____ Date:_____

Directions: Read the text, and answer the questions.

A traditional economic system follows customs. People work the same way as their ancestors did. They use tradition to control day-to-day life. Many traditional economies are based on farming. Others focus on hunting, fishing, or gathering. All the people in the society do similar work. There are not many different jobs. The society produces enough to live, and there is little surplus.

Ancient societies were traditional economic systems at first. The economies changed as they grew. There are still traditional economies in the world today. This suits the society. There is little waste.

Herding reindeer is a form of traditional farming.

1. How do members of a traditional economic system make economic decisions?
   a. They talk about their ideas.
   b. They follow the ways of their ancestors.
   c. They talk to a judge.
   d. They copy the ideas of other societies.

2. What are the bases of traditional economic systems? Circle all that apply.
   a. hunting
   b. farming
   c. gathering
   d. selling

3. Why were early ancient societies traditional economic systems?
   a. They were not interested in trying new economic systems.
   b. They were large societies, so people needed to know their jobs.
   c. They offered people wider choices of different roles or jobs.
   d. They had to focus on getting enough food to survive.

Name:_____ **Date:**_____

Directions: Read the text, and answer the questions.

Traditional economic systems follow the traditions of the past. They don't change easily. This means that the society is slow to learn new ways or better ways to accomplish tasks.

When people from traditional societies meet members of other kinds of economies and societies, they may see new methods. They discover new resources. They can trade for new tools so they can hunt or farm more efficiently. This may lead to surpluses and more flexibility. Often, the traditional society begins to become a mixed economy. Most people will continue to farm or hunt. But some people learn new jobs. The people begin to want new goods and services.

Early Inuit were a traditional society.

1. Why don't traditional economic systems change easily?

   a. They see how other people complete tasks.

   b. They try new methods when they see them.

   c. They follow the rules and ways of the past.

   d. They have a system that few people understand.

2. Imagine that people from a traditional economic society meet people from a different society. Based on the text, what might happen?

   a. They may learn better ways to farm or hunt.

   b. They may avoid the new people.

   c. They may stay exactly the same.

   d. They may plant crops.

3. What do you think a society needs before it can diversify jobs and goods? Explain.

   _____

   _____

   _____

Economics

Name: _____ Date: _____

Directions: Study the map, and answer the questions..

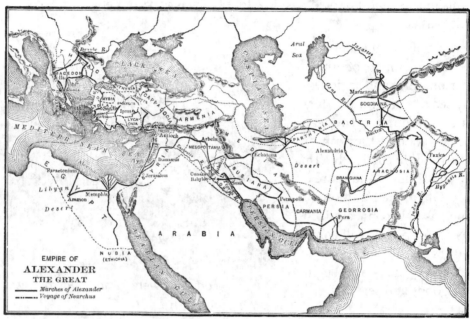

Empire of Alexander the Great

Alexander the Great's empire led to increased trade and an exchange of culture and knowledge.

1. Look at the map. What do you think the differences would be across this large empire?

   a. types of animals   **c.** climate

   b. grains produced on farms **d.** all the above

2. Why would this empire lead to changes for many societies?

   _____

   _____

   _____

3. How would you feel if a trader offered you money, and you had never seen money before?

   _____

   _____

   _____

51398—180 Days of Social Studies

Name: _____ Date: _____

Directions: Read the text, and study the images. Answer the questions.

Economics

   Money is used as a way to measure the value of something. It is easier than bartering goods or services.

Some coins honored leaders. This is Alexander the Great.

early American colonial money

The Chinese made the first paper money. It was lighter than coins.

1. Why do you think money made trading easier?

   a. There was only one type of currency.

   b. People didn't have to trade goods.

   c. People liked carrying money.

   d. People liked to have many different types of goods available.

2. Why did paper money replace many coins?

   _____

   _____

   _____

3. What would you put on the front and back of a coin? Why?

   _____

   _____

   _____

Economics

Name: _____ **Date:** _____

Directions: Study the map, and answer the question.

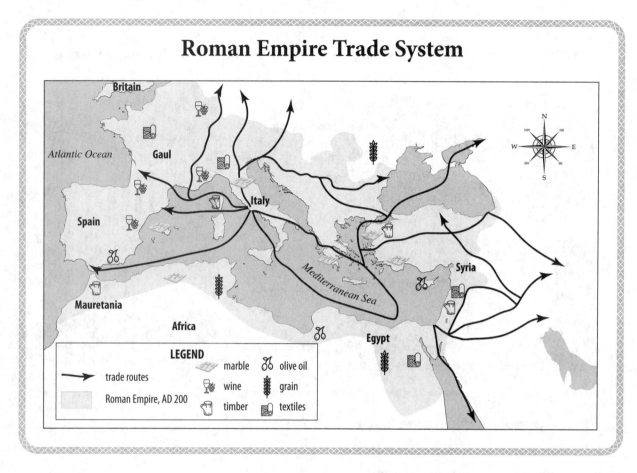

Roman Empire Trade System

LEGEND

→ trade routes

▨ Roman Empire, AD 200

◿ marble
🍷 wine
🖐 timber
🍒 olive oil
🌾 grain
▨ textiles

1. Based on the map, what types of goods were traded with the Roman Empire? What were the main goods traded in Spain? In Egypt?

_____

_____

_____

_____

_____

_____

_____

_____

Name: _____ Date: _____

Directions: Read the text, and answer the questions.

The Kingdom of Kush developed in Africa. The main cities of Kush lay along the Nile, White Nile, and Blue Nile rivers. Around 1070 BC, the people broke away from Egypt and made their own kingdom. They flourished for over 1,400 years.

They depended on metals like gold and iron. Gold was used for jewelry and art and was traded with other people. Iron was used to make strong tools and weapons. Kushites also produced fine pottery and built pyramids.

Women were important in Kush society and could be leaders. The people of Kush believed in many of the Egyptian gods. The Egyptian goddess Isis, the goddess of magic and motherhood, became a powerful part of the Kush religion. This helped to remind the people that women were powerful and important, too.

from a city in Kush

1. Based on the text, what geographic features were important for the growth of Kush as a powerful civilization?

   a. fertile rivers

   b. mountains

   c. cornfields

   d. deserts

2. Why were metals important in Kush?

   a. They could be mined.

   b. They could be used to build pyramids.

   c. They could be used for jewelry and tool making.

   d. They could be used to make pottery.

3. What is the most likely reason that Kushites built pyramids?

   a. They did not want to invent their own buildings.

   b. They used to be part of Egypt, so they learned Egyptian building.

   c. They thought pyramids were the best places to store their pottery.

   d. They thought the goddess of the Nile expected it.

History

Name:_____ Date:_____

Directions: Read the text, and answer the questions.

Kush was part of Egypt for many years and followed the Egyptian religion. It was a polytheistic religion. It had many gods. For many years, the capital of Kush was Napata. The center of Napata was a sandstone butte rising from the desert. The butte was called Jebel Barkal. The Kushites believed that it was the birthplace of Amun. Amun was seen as a king of the gods. Therefore, Jebel Barkal was a powerful place to build a capital city. However, the Kushites also had some of their own gods. One of them was Apedemak, the god of war. In the sixth century AD, Christian missionaries came to Kush. They began to teach stories from the Bible. Christianity became popular across northern Africa. Many of the people of Kush embraced this religion.

Jebel Barkal

1. Why might the Kushites originally have believed in many Egyptian gods?

   a. They did not want to invent their own.

   b. They already worshipped the Egyptian gods.

   c. It was an interesting religion.

   d. They didn't understand any other religion.

2. Why did Christian missionaries go to Kush?

   a. They needed to leave their home countries.

   b. They wanted to live in a hot place.

   c. They wanted to teach other people about their religion.

   d. They wanted to live near a river.

3. Based on the text, why do you think Jebel Barkal became a special place?

   a. It looked different or mystical because the land around it was flat.

   b. It was an interesting place to visit.

   c. It was close to their homes and gave a center to the city.

   d. The god Amun was very important to the people.

Name:_____ Date:_____

Directions: Look at the graphic, and answer the questions.

1. What is a monotheistic religion?

   a. A religion that only talks about one thing.

   b. A religion with only one god.

   c. A religion with many gods.

   d. A religion for people who don't like laws.

2. Why was the Israelites' religion unique in the world at that time?

   a. It was based on stories.

   b. It was based on the culture of Europe.

   c. It was monotheistic.

   d. It had very few rules.

3. Why were the commandments so important to the Israelites?

   _____

   _____

   _____

History

Name:_____ Date:_____

Directions: Read the timeline, and answer the questions.

Israel Timeline

1300 BC	63 BC	AD 66–70	AD 614–1071	AD 1099	AD 1187
Israelites start a nation.	Romans conquer Israel.	Jewish people revolt against the Romans.	At various times, Persian, Byzantine Empire, and Muslim forces capture Jerusalem.	Christian Crusaders conquer Jerusalem.	Saladin of Egypt captures Jerusalem.

1. Based on this timeline, what can you infer about the city of Jerusalem?

   a. People who live there are revolutionaries.

   b. It is a large and busy city.

   c. Many people have wanted to control it.

   d. It is a new city.

2. About how many years ago did the ancient Hebrews start a nation? How did you determine your answer?

   _____

   _____

   _____

   _____

3. Jerusalem is a holy site for Jewish people, Christians, and Muslims. Could it be shared by all people? Explain your thinking.

   _____

   _____

   _____

   _____

   _____

   _____

   _____

51398—180 Days of Social Studies

Name:_____ Date:_____

Directions: Read the text, and study the image. Complete the task.

The Romans destroyed the Second Temple in Jerusalem in AD 70. Only one outer wall was left. This wall still stands today. The Western Wall, or Kotel ha-Ma'aravi, became the holiest spot in Jewish life. It is still visited by thousands of people every day.

The Western Wall is also known as the Wailing Wall.

1. The Romans wanted the people they conquered to follow Roman religion. Why did they destroy an important religious place like the Second Temple? Do you think their plan was effective? Why or why not?

_____

_____

_____

_____

_____

_____

_____

_____

_____

Civics

Name: _____ Date: _____

Directions: Read the text, and circle the best answer for each question.

A *limited* government has established, written laws. They are set out in a document such as a constitution. These laws protect the rights of citizens. They state that all people must obey the laws or be punished. No one is above the law, not even the leaders. It does not matter what their wealth or position is. Some countries that have a constitution and a limited government are the United States, Canada, Germany, and Japan.

An *unlimited* government is governed by a leader who is "above the law." This means that the leader's decisions do not need to follow set laws. He or she has total power and can make the choices he or she wants. The citizens have no say, and they must do what the leader wants. Some countries that have an unlimited government are North Korea and China.

1. What is a limited government?
   a. one in which the president makes all the decisions
   b. one that has established laws that everyone must follow
   c. one in which all must follow the laws, except the leader
   d. one in which a king or queen holds all the power

2. What is an unlimited government?
   a. one where no one is above the law
   b. one where the leader respects and follows the laws
   c. one where a small group of leaders follow the laws
   d. one where the leader has total power

3. Which countries have the same type of government?
   a. the United States, Russia, and Japan
   b. the United States, North Korea, and Japan
   c. the United States, China, and Russia
   d. the United States, Japan, and Germany

51398—180 Days of Social Studies

Name:_____ Date:_____

Directions: Read the text, and study the pictures. Then, answer the questions.

Civics

Like many other countries, the United States has a constitution. The Constitution is an important *document*. It is the *highest law* in the country. And, it is the tool that *limits the powers* of people in government.

The Constitution has three parts:

- The Preamble says who is writing the document and why.

- The Articles set out each branch of the government and describe each branch's purpose and limited power. They also tell about rules for states.

- The Amendments are the parts that were added to the Constitution. They include the Bill of Rights. There are 27 amendments in all, and some limit government.

the U.S. Constitution

1. What is the main reason why the U.S. Constitution is important?

   a. It is a document.

   b. It has a history in our country.

   c. It is the highest law.

   d. It is a law that is written on a document.

2. What part(s) of the Constitution limit(s) government power?

   a. the Preamble

   b. the Preamble and the Amendments

   c. the Articles and the Amendments

   d. the Preamble and the Articles

3. Which part of the Constitution sets out the rules for states?

   a. the Articles

   b. the Preamble

   c. the Amendments

   d. none of the above

Name: _____ Date: _____

Civics

Directions: Look at the graphic, and answer the questions.

Unlimited Power

Nazi Germany
- It was ruled by Hitler and the Nazis during World War II.
- The constitution did not protect the people.
- The leader did not respect the people's rights.
- The leader made his power unlimited, and he hurt and killed people.

Iraq
- It was ruled by Saddam Hussein from 1979 to 2003.
- The constitution did not protect the people.
- The leader did not respect the people's rights.
- The leader made his power unlimited, and he hurt and killed people.

China
- The leaders use their constitution to promote a communist state.
- The country is governed by one party.
- The people do not have certain freedoms.
- It can be dangerous to protest the government.

1. Which of these describes a government with unlimited power?

   a. It cannot ever have a constitution for the country.

   b. It can have a constitution and the leader protects people's rights.

   c. It can have a constitution where the leader has only some power.

   d. It can have a constitution and the leader is all powerful.

2. Tell about the government and its decisions in Nazi Germany.

   _____

   _____

3. How does the government in China promote a communist state?

   _____

   _____

Name: _____ **Date:** _____

Directions: Read the text, and answer the questions.

A constitution states what a government intends to do. The U.S. Constitution limits government power. It sets out how the government is organized. It tells about the relationship between the people and the government. It protects the rights and freedoms of people. It sets laws that keep people safe. Here are some important amendments to the Constitution.

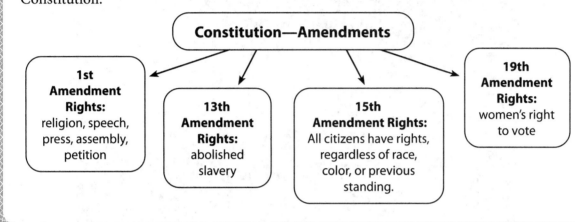

Constitution—Amendments

1st Amendment Rights: religion, speech, press, assembly, petition

13th Amendment Rights: abolished slavery

15th Amendment Rights: All citizens have rights, regardless of race, color, or previous standing.

19th Amendment Rights: women's right to vote

Civics

1. How does the U.S. Constitution protect people? Circle the best answer.

   a. It tells what a government intends to do.

   b. It tells how a government is organized.

   c. It safeguards the rights of the people.

   d. all the above

2. Which of these amendments make it clear that the Constitution is for everyone in our country? Explain.

   _____

   _____

   _____

3. Which of these amendments affects you and your family? Tell why.

   _____

   _____

   _____

Civics

Name:_____ Date:_____

Directions: Read the text, and study the pictures. Then, complete the task.

We live in a country that has a constitution and a limited government. The rights of the people are respected. There are countries where government is unlimited. Their leaders have all the power. The people have little or no say.

American protesters

1. Compare and contrast two government systems: the United States and China. In which would you prefer to live? Why?

_____

_____

_____

_____

_____

_____

_____

_____

_____

Name: _____ **Date:** _____

Directions: Read the text, and answer the questions.

Thematic Map

A thematic map looks at one piece of information. This can be about a topic such as weather, health, or where people live in certain areas. This map shows where most enslaved people lived in Virginia in 1860.

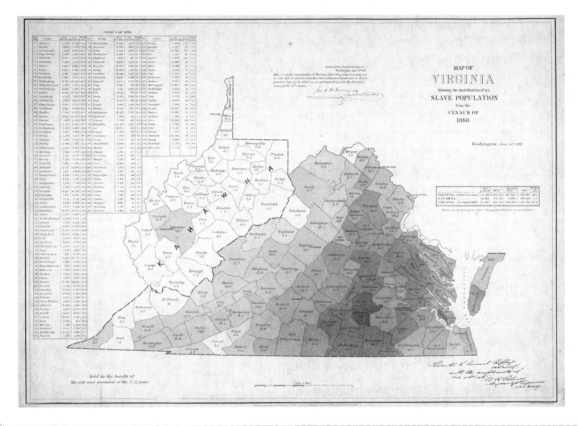

1. What is unique about a thematic map?

   a. directions to various places

   b. information on one topic

   c. the location of landmarks

   d. hills and valleys

2. How could you use a thematic map?

   a. to find directions to someone's house

   b. to see where the closest store is

   c. to find out what the tallest mountain is

   d. to see the rainfall amount across the United States

Geography

Name: _____ Date: _____

Directions: Read the text, and look at the map. Answer the questions.

We can use thematic maps to look at patterns. For example, researchers might compare a map that shows flu outbreaks in 2015 to a map of the same information for 2018. This helps them see how the information changed. They may then compare that information to a map showing where the most flu shots were used in the same area to look for patterns and connections.

Thematic maps have been used in research for a long time. In 1854, Dr. John Snow created the first thematic map to find out about a disease that was spreading in London, England. He saw a pattern of where the sickness was starting. He found that many people were getting sick close to a certain water pump. Dr. Snow had them stop using that pump, and new cases of the sickness stopped. Using thematic maps, he found the cause of how that disease was spread.

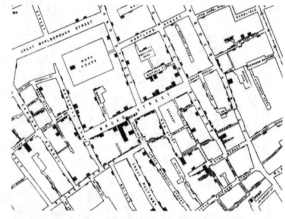

Dr. Snow's map, 1854

1. How do thematic maps help people look at patterns?

   a. They show the same information from various times or places.

   b. They show different information on the same map.

   c. The maps are not often used to see patterns.

   d. The maps are used to show directions.

2. How did a thematic map help Dr. Snow know more about the spread of a disease?

   a. He was able to learn that there was a disease spreading in London.

   b. He was able to learn where the disease started by mapping the illness.

   c. The thematic map helped him see how much rainfall the city had that year.

   d. The thematic map showed him where people were living in the city of London.

3. Suppose you had thematic weather maps from the summers of 2015 and 2017. What would these maps tell you?

   a. which states are normally cooler in summer

   b. which states have the most snow in winter

   c. how much cloud cover there was in the summer

   d. what state had the hottest summer in 2016

Name:_____ Date:_____

Directions: Study the map, and answer the questions.

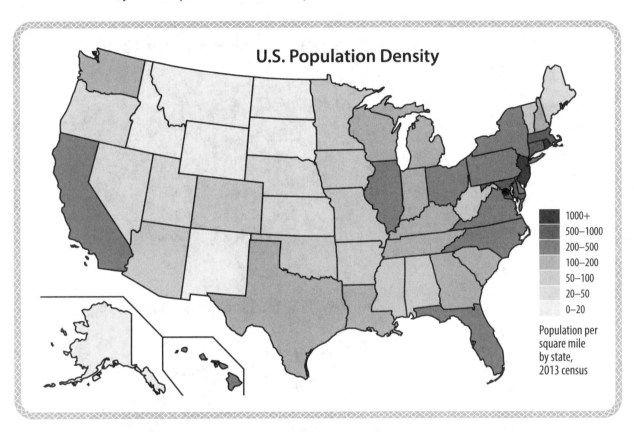

U.S. Population Density

1000+
500–1000
200–500
100–200
50–100
20–50
0–20

Population per square mile by state, 2013 census

Geography

1. Population density is the average number of people living in an area. Which of the following states has one of the highest population densities?

   a. Nevada

   b. New Jersey

   c. Alabama

   d. Washington

2. Why do the central northern states have fewer people per square mile?

   a. They are larger states with a lot of people.

   b. They are smaller states with lots people.

   c. They are larger states with fewer people.

   d. They are smaller states with fewer people.

3. Locate your state. What is the population density there? Which states have population densities similar to your state's?

   _____

   _____

   _____

Geography

Name:_____ Date:_____

Directions: Study the maps, and answer the questions.

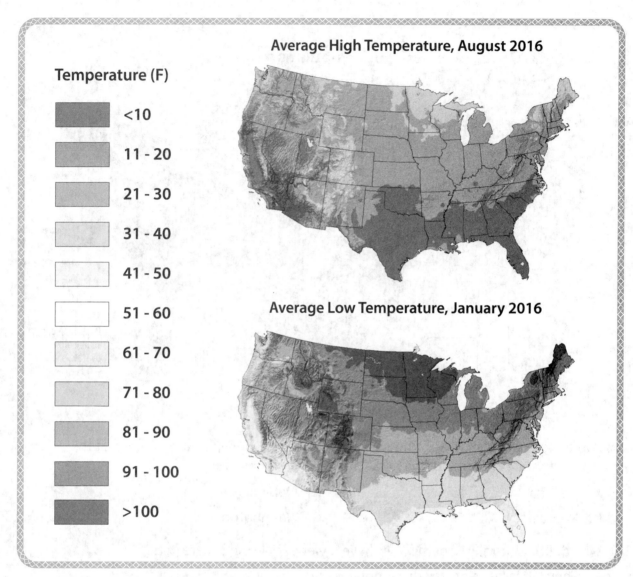

Temperature (F)

<10

11 - 20

21 - 30

31 - 40

41 - 50

51 - 60

61 - 70

71 - 80

81 - 90

91 - 100

>100

Average High Temperature, August 2016

Average Low Temperature, January 2016

1. Which of these states has the coolest summer and coldest winter?

   a. Texas

   c. Minnesota

   b. Utah

   d. California

2. Which state was the hottest in the summer? Which was the coldest in the winter?

   _____

3. Describe the climate of the state you live in.

   _____

   _____

Name: _____ **Date:** _____

Directions: Draw a plan of your school.

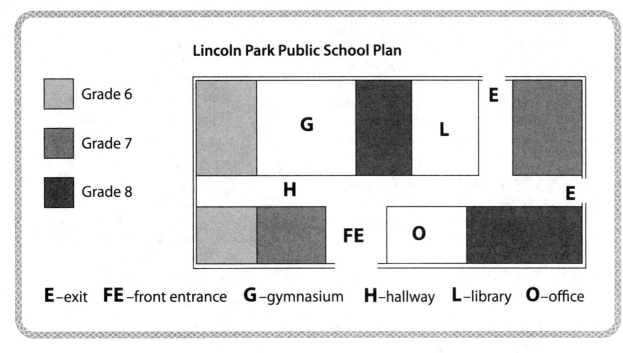

Lincoln Park Public School Plan

Grade 6

Grade 7

Grade 8

E–exit   **FE**–front entrance   **G**–gymnasium   **H**–hallway   **L**–library   **O**–office

1. Draw the basic shape of your school, and mark off the classrooms. Make a legend showing the different classes and areas in your school. Color and label the map to match.

Economics

Name: _____ Date: _____

Directions: Read the text, and answer the questions.

Market economies depend on the wants and needs of individuals and companies. Governments don't intervene in a pure market economy. Everything is determined by supply and demand. Consumers buy what they want and can afford. Producers provide the goods or services they wish.

When the demand goes up companies make more, so the supply increases. But if the price is too high, people stop buying. Then the demand goes down. A market economy equilibrium is reached when the supply meets the demand for a product.

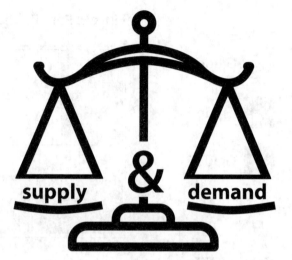

Equilibrium is balance between opposing forces.

1. Who or what partly determines what happens in a market economy?

    a. consumers

    b. governments

    c. traditionalists

    d. corporations

2. Why does the demand for an item go down when the price goes up?

    a. There are fewer available.

    b. The company doesn't have enough.

    c. People won't pay the high price.

    d. There are many left over.

3. When do people stop buying?

    a. when equilibrium is reached

    b. when the supply is too high

    c. when the price is too high

    d. when supply is low

Name:_____ Date:_____

Directions: Read the text, and answer the questions.

Economics

A market economy has little or no government control. Most goods and services are privately owned. That means that people or companies own them. Any profits from these goods or services belong to the owner. However, the amount of profit depends on the market forces and balance.

Consumers want to pay as little as possible. The producer wants to charge as much as possible. Similarly, an employer needs to hire competent workers but wants to pay lower wages. At the same time, competent workers want to earn as much as possible. In a market economy, a balance is found without government controls such as a minimum wage.

1. Who makes profits from selling goods or services?

   a. the purchaser   **c.** the government

   b. the consumer   **d.** the producer

2. Why do employers want to pay lower wages?

   a. so they can hire the best people

   b. so they don't use much of their profit

   c. so they keep their employees happy

   d. so they don't need lots of cash

3. What is a minimum wage?

   a. government control of the lowest amount a person can be paid

   b. the minimum price for a produced good

   c. a way to make sure that a company can make a large profit

   d. all the above

Economics

Name: _____ Date: _____

Directions: Look at the graphic, and answer the questions.

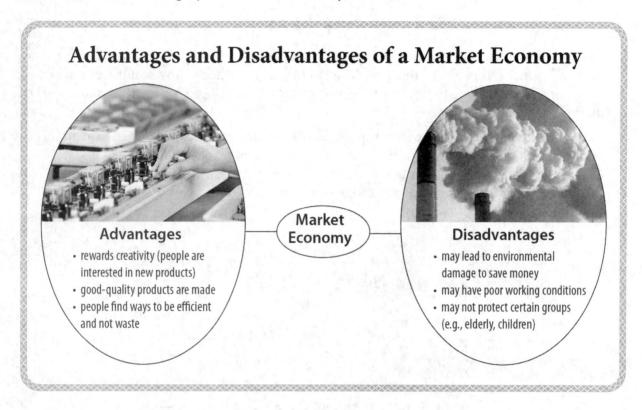

1. Why do market economies usually lead to good-quality products?

   a. The workers are proud of their work.

   b. The companies want to save money.

   c. Consumers won't pay for poor-quality products.

   d. People have good ideas.

2. Why do companies look for ways to be efficient and not waste resources?

   _____

   _____

   _____

3. How might poor working conditions affect products? Explain.

   _____

   _____

   _____

51398—180 Days of Social Studies

Name: _____ Date: _____

Directions: Read the text, and study the graphic. Answer the questions.

Economics

> The Constitution supports a market economy. It also lets the government make some economic laws. This means the United States is not a pure market economy. Instead, it uses a mixed economy.

The federal government can...	
• regulate commerce with foreign nations	Article I, Section 8
• coin money and punish counterfeiters	Article I, Sections 8 and 10

Free markets are protected by...	
• copyright protection for science and the arts	Article I, Section 8
• contract protection	Article I, Section 9
• not allowing states to tax imports or exports	Article I, Section 10
• not allowing states to tax goods from other states	Article I, Sections 9 and 10
• private property protection	Amendments IV, V, and XIV

1. Based on the text, how are free markets protected?

    a. non regulated trade with other countries

    b. copyright protection

    c. counterfeiter protection

    d. taxation on goods from other states

2. Why do you think it's important for the federal government to be in charge of creating all the money for the country? Explain.

    _____

    _____

    _____

3. Why is private property important for you?

    _____

    _____

    _____

    _____

Economics

Name: _____ **Date:** _____

Directions: Look at the images, and answer the question.

Types of Businesses

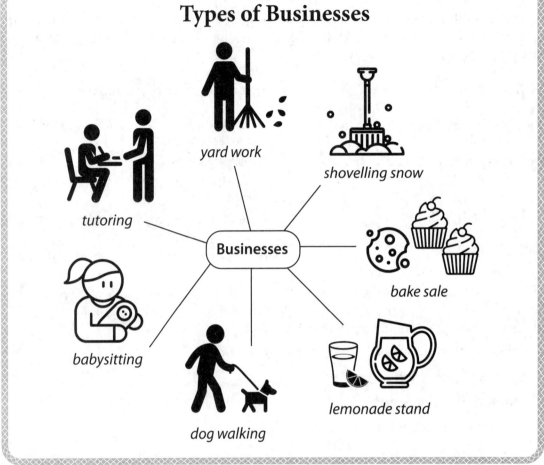

tutoring

yard work

shovelling snow

Businesses

bake sale

babysitting

dog walking

lemonade stand

1. Pick one of these businesses to develop and run. Describe your business, and explain why it is an example of a free market business.

_____

_____

_____

_____

_____

_____

_____

Name: _____ **Date:** _____

Directions: Read the text, and answer the questions.

Ancient Greece was not one country like it is today. Instead, it was made up of several city-states. Each city-state had a central city. This city ruled the land around the city. Each city-state had its own government. A king or tyrant ruled some city-states. An oligarchy (a group of powerful men) ruled other city-states.

Poseidon

The city-state of Athens was unique. Athenians invented the idea of democracy. Athenian male citizens ruled Athens. Women, children, enslaved people, and foreigners could not vote.

Religion was also very important in the Greek city-states. They had many gods. They built temples for their gods. They also told stories about the adventures of the gods, goddesses, and the human heroes. For example, Poseidon was the god of the sea, horses, storms, and earthquakes. He was a bad-tempered and greedy god.

1. What made ancient Greece different from modern Greece?

    a. It had large, fertile rivers.

    b. It had many gods.

    c. It had city-states.

    d. It was one big country.

2. How were city-states governed?

    a. Male citizens voted.

    b. A king controlled some city-states.

    c. A group of powerful men ran some city-states.

    d. all the above

3. What characteristic made Poseidon a good god for storms and earthquakes?

    a. He enjoyed having fun.

    b. He was often angry.

    c. He was calm.

    d. He was generous.

History

History

Name: _____ Date: _____

Directions: Read the text, and answer the questions

> Sparta was a very powerful Greek city-state because all the men trained to be brave warriors. Spartan boys went to harsh schools when they reached age seven. The boys lived at the school. They were often beaten and given little food so they would become tough. When the boys reached age 20, they joined the army. Girls also went to school. They were expected to exercise and be strong and fit so they would have warrior sons. Two kings and a council of older men ruled the city-state. The Spartan men were all soldiers. The hands-on work was done by enslaved people called Helots.
>
>
>
> *The Spartans honored brave soldiers.*

1. What does the picture tell you about Sparta?

   a. Soldiers were important.

   b. The men did all the manual work.

   c. The men kept the women company.

   d. The men ran the schools.

2. What was a woman's role in Sparta?

   a. to marry and have many warrior sons

   b. to become a brave soldier

   c. to help her sons with homework

   d. to look after the gods

3. Based on the text, how do you think Sparta was ruled?

   a. an oligarchy

   b. a tyranny

   c. a democracy

   d. a matriarchy

Name:_____ Date:_____

Directions: Look at the graphic, and answer the questions.

History

Roles in Ancient Athens

Boys and Men in Athens

- Boys began school at age seven and studied math, reading, writing, debating, and music.
- They could explore the city.
- Men had many different jobs.
- They debated and voted on how to run the city-state.

Girls and Women in Athens

- Girls did not go to school.
- Girls learned at home how to look after a house.
- Middle- and upper-class women spent most of their time at home.
- Husbands did not allow women to leave home.

- The Athenians followed the Greek religion and believed in many gods and goddesses.
- They respected Athena the goddess of wisdom, war, and civilization.
- They used enslaved people to do a lot of work.

1. Why didn't Athenian girls go to school?

   a. They didn't want to learn to read and write.

   b. They used enslaved people for help.

   c. They were not allowed to go to school.

   d. They didn't want to be with the boys.

2. Pale faces were a sign of beauty for women in Athens. Why were the women's faces pale?

   a. They wore hats to protect their faces.

   b. The goddesses had pale faces.

   c. The women rarely went outside.

   d. The women worked very hard.

3. Athenian men kept their wives and daughters in the house. Newborn girls were not wanted. What can you infer about Athenian attitudes toward women?

   _____

   _____

History

Name:_____ Date:_____

Directions: Read the web, and answer the questions.

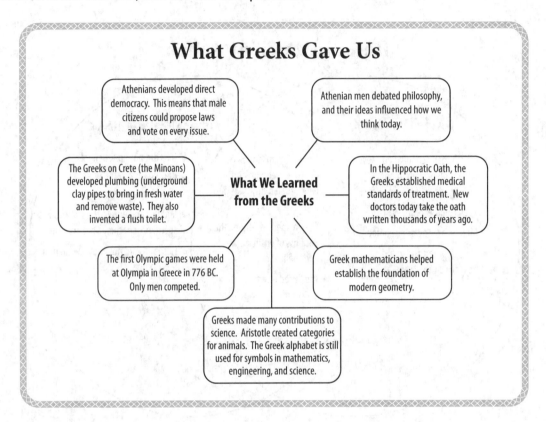

What Greeks Gave Us

Athenians developed direct democracy. This means that male citizens could propose laws and vote on every issue.

Athenian men debated philosophy, and their ideas influenced how we think today.

The Greeks on Crete (the Minoans) developed plumbing (underground clay pipes to bring in fresh water and remove waste). They also invented a flush toilet.

What We Learned from the Greeks

In the Hippocratic Oath, the Greeks established medical standards of treatment. New doctors today take the oath written thousands of years ago.

The first Olympic games were held at Olympia in Greece in 776 BC. Only men competed.

Greek mathematicians helped establish the foundation of modern geometry.

Greeks made many contributions to science. Aristotle created categories for animals. The Greek alphabet is still used for symbols in mathematics, engineering, and science.

1. What is direct democracy?

   a. elected officials representing a group of people

   b. a way for a king to rule a city-state

   c. citizens discuss, vote, and create laws

   d. the type of democracy used in the United States

2. Think about the activities of the ancient Greeks. What can you infer about their ability to provide for their basic needs?

   _____

   _____

   _____

3. Which of the Greek contributions do you think is the most significant? Why?

   _____

   _____

   _____

Name: _____ Date: _____

Directions: Read the text, and study the images. Complete the task.

Socrates was an Athenian philosopher. His ideas shaped western thought. He taught his students to use questions and discussion. Socrates made some people angry because of his beliefs.

The Spartan king Leonidas led about 7,000 soldiers at the Battle of Thermopylae. They fought more than 10 times as many Persian enemies. Leonidas and his 300-man bodyguard refused to retreat and were killed.

1. Compare and contrast the city-states of Athens and Sparta.

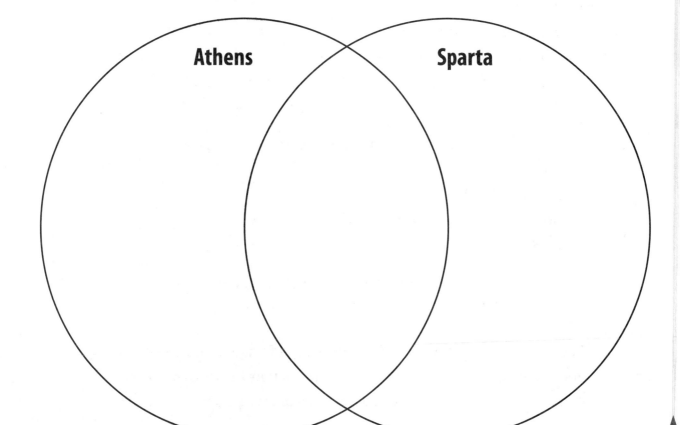

Athens

Sparta

Name:_____ **Date:**_____

Civics

Directions: Read the text, and circle the best answer for each question.

In Russia, the president and the prime minister both work at running the country. But the president has complete power. He can veto any law or decision that is made by the government. He can make any law without checking with other officials in the government. He can change any law that is made by the government. He has complete immunity—he cannot be brought to court.

The Russian constitution sets out how the government is run. There are three branches of government. The president is in charge of the executive branch, which is the most powerful. There is also a legislative branch (the appointed Federation Council and the elected Duma) and a judicial branch (the courts).

Vladimir Putin, president of Russia

1. Which statement is true?

   a. Congress may override the Russian president's veto.

   b. The Russian president can create laws independently.

   c. The Russian prime minister can make laws independently.

   d. The Russian prime minister has the right to veto any law.

2. What would be done if the Russian president committed a crime against the people?

   a. He would be charged by the police.

   b. He would not be charged of a crime.

   c. He would be charged by military police.

   d. He would be brought to a court of law.

3. How are the branches of Russian government similar to those of the American government?

   a. Both countries have a House of Representatives.

   b. Both countries have a president and a vice president.

   c. Both countries have checks and balances to limit power of government.

   d. Both countries have executive, judicial, and legislative branches.

Name: _____ Date: _____

Directions: Read the text, and study the picture. Then, answer the questions.

The Russian constitution also sets out the freedoms and rights of people. It lists rights such as these:

- People are equal before the law.
- People have the right to life.
- People have freedom of ideas, speech, and religion. They have the right to peaceful assembly without weapons.
- People can work and own property.
- The government pays for medical services.
- People have a right to education.

However, the Human Rights Watch reports that Russia has repressed many human rights. These include freedom of press (news, Internet), speech, and assembly. Troops backed by Russia have also abused human rights in Ukraine.

1. Which statement about the Russian constitution is true?
   a. It limits the power of the government.
   b. It states that people have freedom of speech.
   c. It prevents the right to education.
   d. It states that citizens cannot own their own houses.

2. What are two services that are provided to all citizens for free?
   a. housing and food services
   b. transportation and housing
   c. medical services and schooling
   d. travel and office services

3. How is the information from the Human Rights Watch different from the Russian constitution?
   a. It tells us that the president is respecting the rights of all the people.
   b. It tells us that the prime minister is respecting the rights of all people.
   c. It tells us that there is repression of the freedom of press, speech, and assembly.
   d. It tells us that the president has restricted people's freedoms.

Civics

Name:_____ **Date:**_____

Directions: Study the web. Then, answer the questions.

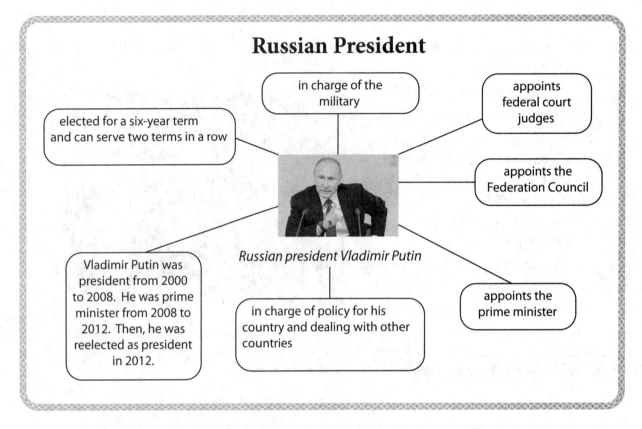

Russian President

in charge of the military

appoints federal court judges

elected for a six-year term and can serve two terms in a row

appoints the Federation Council

Russian president Vladimir Putin

Vladimir Putin was president from 2000 to 2008. He was prime minister from 2008 to 2012. Then, he was reelected as president in 2012.

in charge of policy for his country and dealing with other countries

appoints the prime minister

1. How long can a person be the president of Russia?

   a. two terms of four years

   b. one term of six years

   c. two terms of six years

   d. two terms of four years

2. The American government wants to make a trade deal with Russia. Who would our government deal with? Why?

   _____

   _____

3. In 2014, the Russian army invaded the Crimea region in Ukraine. Who was responsible for this action? Why?

   _____

   _____

   _____

Name:_____ Date:_____

Directions: Look at the chart, read the text, and compare the information. Then, answer the questions.

U.S. and Russian Government Systems			
Country	Executive	Legislative	Judicial
United States	President Vice President Executive Office Cabinet The president executes laws written by Congress. He appoints leaders of agencies. He is the commander of the military forces. He has limited power.	Congress is made up of the House of Representatives and the Senate. Its most important job is making laws. It can also impeach government officials. It is part of the "checks and balances" system.	The Supreme Court is in control of this branch. They interpret and apply the laws. Any citizen can be tried in a court of law.
Russia	President Prime Minister Administration Deputies Ministers The president is elected. The president appoints all officials in the executive branch. He is the commander of the military forces. He has complete power.	The Federal Assembly is made up of the Federal Council and the Duma. The Duma is in charge of finances. The Federation Council looks after relations between the federal and state governments. The legislature is very weak because the president has so much power.	This branch is made up of the Supreme Court and the Constitutional Court. The justice system is very weak. People's rights are not always respected.

Civics

1. Based on the text, how are the presidents of these two countries different?
   a. One is the leader of the military forces, and the other is not.
   b. One appoints officials in the executive branch, and the other does not.
   c. One has limited power, and the other does not.
   d. none of the above

2. What power(s) does our legislative branch have that the Russian branch does not? Explain.

   _____

   _____

3. Pretend you were falsely charged with a crime. Would you prefer to go to an American court or a Russian court? Why?

   _____

   _____

Civics

Name: _____ Date: _____

Directions: Read the text, and study the pictures. Then, complete the task.

Both the United States and Russia have constitutions. These documents state the rights and freedoms of the people. The president of the United States is not above the law. The president of Russia has the power to make or change laws as he chooses.

American news reporter

The Russian president controls all news stations.

1. Compare and contrast how rights and freedoms are different for the people of the United States and the people of Russia. How could this affect the relationship between the countries?

_____

_____

_____

_____

_____

_____

_____

_____

_____

_____

_____

51398—180 Days of Social Studies

Geography

Name:_____ Date:_____

Directions: Read the text, and answer the questions.

Physical geography plays a key role in where people choose to settle. In early settlements, people had to be able to grow crops and raise animals. This meant that good soil was important. Other key factors were access to water, flat land, and being near useful resources such as wood. Early towns needed to be close to waterways for travel and trade. As things advanced, railroads and roads became more important. Climate is also very important. Areas that are very hot or very cold are not ideal for settlements.

early settlers in Nebraska

1. Which of the following factors make an area right for a settlement?

   a. average weather

   b. access to resources

   c. access to entertainment

   d. tall mountains

2. Why were waterways a key factor for early settlements?

   a. They were good for transporting goods for sale.

   b. They were nice to look at for the settlers.

   c. Settlers could sell the water.

   d. They helped people build roads and railroads.

3. Why was rich soil important for successful settlements?

   a. Plants and flowers make for a nicer community.

   b. Soil was used to build roadways and walking trails.

   c. It makes it easier to grow food.

   d. It makes it easier for travel.

© *Shell Education*   *51398—180 Days of Social Studies*

Geography

Name:_____ Date:_____

Directions: Read the chart, and answer the questions.

Factors Affecting Population Density		
Factor	**High Density**	**Low Density**
relief (shape and height of land)	Low-lying, flat land encourages settlement. It is easier to build on.	Land that is high and rugged is harder to build on.
soil	Rich and fertile soils are best for farming. In early settlements, this was key for a survival.	If soil in the area isn't good for growing crops, it is less likely to be settled.
climate	A moderate climate is best for human populations.	Areas too hot or too cold, or with extreme weather, are not as good for settlements.
resources	Places rich in resources are often most settled. Resources include wood, oil, coal, fish, and animals for hunting.	Areas with fewer resources are not ideal places to build a settlement.
water	Access to fresh drinking water is important for human settlement. In early settlements, waterways were also helpful for travel and trade.	Places without access to water are less populated. While access to rivers for travel and trade is less important in modern times, drinking water is vital.
vegetation	Places where it is easy to remove unwanted vegetation make it easier to raise crops and animals.	Areas with thick vegetation are less likely to support settlements easily.

1. Based on the chart, which factor makes constructing homes easier?

   a. fertile soil

   b. low, flat land

   c. moderate climate

   d. all the above

2. Why is climate a key factor for new settlements?

   a. Areas with moderate weather are good for settling.

   b. It is easier to remove vegetation to build on land.

   c. People like to settle where it is hot.

   d. Hot and cold areas make for predictable weather.

3. What role did rivers play in early towns?

   a. provided recreational activities

   b. helped the climate stay moderate

   c. created wet ground for building on

   d. provided a method to travel and trade

51398—180 Days of Social Studies

© *Shell Education*

Name: _____   Date: _____

Directions: Study the map, and answer the questions.

Geography

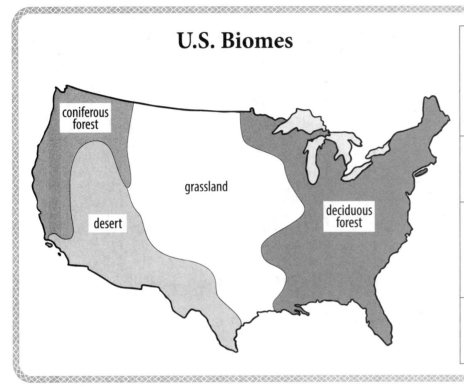

U.S. Biomes

coniferous forest

grassland

desert

deciduous forest

Desert: A dry area with less than 20 inches of rain a year. There are four major types of desert: hot and dry, semi-arid, coastal, and cold.

Coniferous Forest: An area where the rainfall and climate support this type of forest.

Grassland: An area where the average rainfall is enough to support grass and grain growth but very few trees.

Deciduous Forest: An area where the rainfall and climate support this type of forest.

1. Which biome covers most of the Midwest region of the United States?

   a. deciduous forest

   b. desert

   c. coniferous forest

   d. grassland

2. Most of the areas near the coastlines are forest-type biomes. Why do you think that is?

_____

_____

_____

3. How does the amount of rainfall affect the plants that grow in each biome?

_____

_____

_____

Geography

Name: _____ Date: _____

Directions: Study the graphic, and answer the questions.

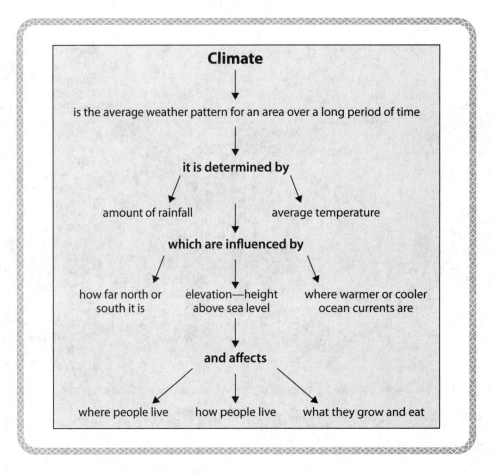

Climate

↓

is the average weather pattern for an area over a long period of time

↓

it is determined by

amount of rainfall   average temperature

which are influenced by

how far north or   elevation—height   where warmer or cooler
south it is   above sea level   ocean currents are

and affects

where people live   how people live   what they grow and eat

1. Why is climate information based on many years and not just months?

   a. Climate frequently changes.

   b. Climate needs to measure time.

   c. The latitude of an area changes over time.

   d. Weather patterns develop over time.

2. What is the difference between weather and climate?

   _____

   _____

3. What is the climate for your state? Why do you think it is that way?

   _____

   _____

Name:_____ Date:_____

Directions: Look at the map, and fill in the chart.

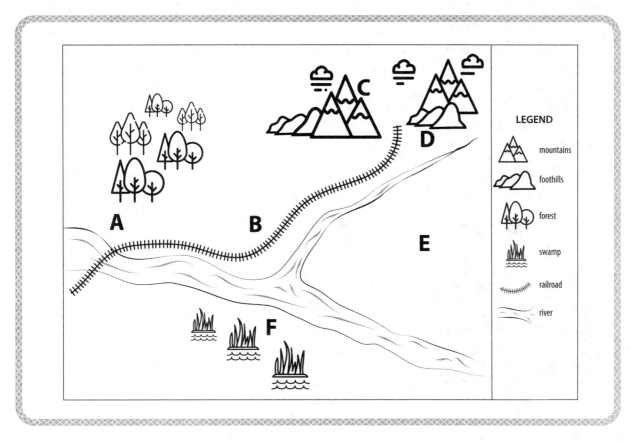

LEGEND

mountains

foothills

forest

swamp

railroad

river

1. For each location, describe what is good and bad about each area for a settlement. In the chart, identify which area you think is best for settlement.

A	
B	
C	
D	
E	
F	

Name:_____ Date:_____

Directions: Read the text, and answer the questions.

Economics

Command economies are run by a central power. This is usually the government. The economy does not adjust based on supply and demand. The government controls most decisions. The government decides how to use resources. It decides how to distribute resources. It controls prices and wages. There is no private property. In some places, citizens are told what their jobs will be. Sometimes, the government controls major resources but lets other parts be freer. Communist countries often have command economies. The amount of government control varies between countries.

Fidel Castro

Mao Zedong

Vladimir Lenin

1. Who determines what happens in a command economy?

   a. consumers

   b. governments

   c. traditionalists

   d. producers

2. Why might the amount of government control vary?

   a. Countries have different histories and traditions.

   b. A new leader takes power and has new ideas.

   c. Countries have different resources and needs.

   d. all the above

3. What replaces the law of supply and demand in a command economy?

   a. no private property

   b. communist countries

   c. government decisions

   d. planned jobs

90

Name: _____ **Date:** _____

Directions: Read the chart, and answer the questions.

Advantages and Disadvantages of a Command Economy	
Advantages	**Disadvantages**
• resources can be directed wherever there is need • people know what to do and where to work • people have employment security • emergencies (disaster, war) can be quickly addressed • mostly equal distribution of wealth • free education, health care, and other services to benefit the common good, not profits	• little incentive to be innovative • little reason to be efficient • slow, long-distance decision-making • supports needs but not necessarily wants • inefficient factories may stay open • reduces personal freedoms • may misjudge what is needed, so may end up with useless goods

Economics

1. Why is there little incentive to be innovative in a command economy?

   a. Employees are not skilled.

   b. The government does not listen to you.

   c. Your boss wants you to do your job.

   d. You don't know what to do.

2. Based on the text, what are advantages of a command economy?

   a. little reason to be efficient

   b. employment security

   c. unequal distribution of wealth

   d. slow decision-making

3. Based on the text, what freedoms are likely missing in a command economy? Circle all that apply.

   a. choice of job

   b. personal freedom

   c. freedom of religion

   d. choice of where to live

Economics

Name:_____ Date:_____

Directions: Study the maps, and answer the questions.

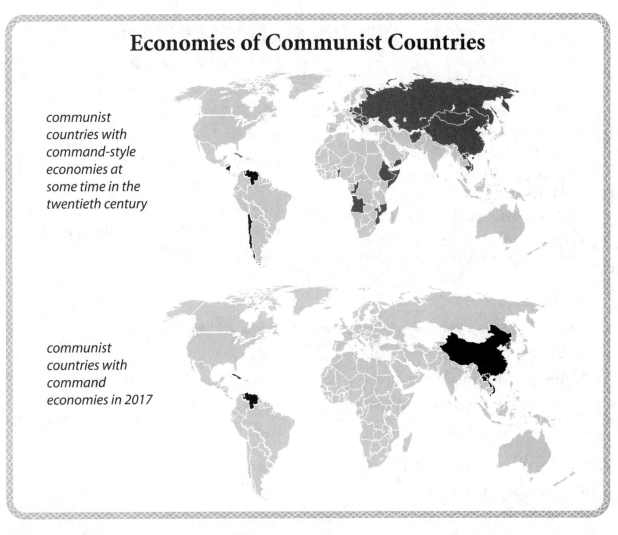

Economies of Communist Countries

communist countries with command-style economies at some time in the twentieth century

communist countries with command economies in 2017

1. Which continent did not have a command economy in the twentieth century?

   a. Europe

   b. North America

   c. Africa

   d. Australia

2. Which continent had the most people living in a command economy in the twentieth century?

   a. South America

   b. North America

   c. Asia

   d. Africa

3. Why are there fewer command economies today?

   _____

   _____

Name:_____ Date:_____

Directions: Study the pie charts, and read the text. Answer the questions.

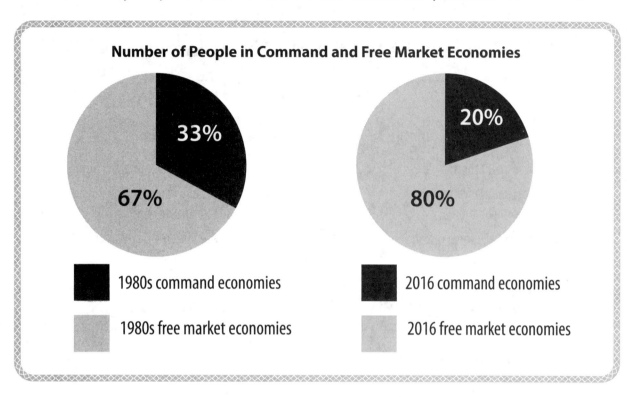

Number of People in Command and Free Market Economies

33%

67%

20%

80%

1980s command economies

1980s free market economies

2016 command economies

2016 free market economies

1. Why has the percentage of people in free market economies increased?

   a. Command economies are popular on some continents.

   b. Free market economies don't work well.

   c. Some command economies have become free market economies.

   d. Some free market economies have become command economies.

2. Describe the change between the 1980s and 2016.

   _____

   _____

3. Where does the United States fit on these pie charts? Why?

   _____

   _____

   _____

Economics

Name:_____ Date:_____

Directions: Study the Venn diagram, and answer the question.

Command and Free Market Economics

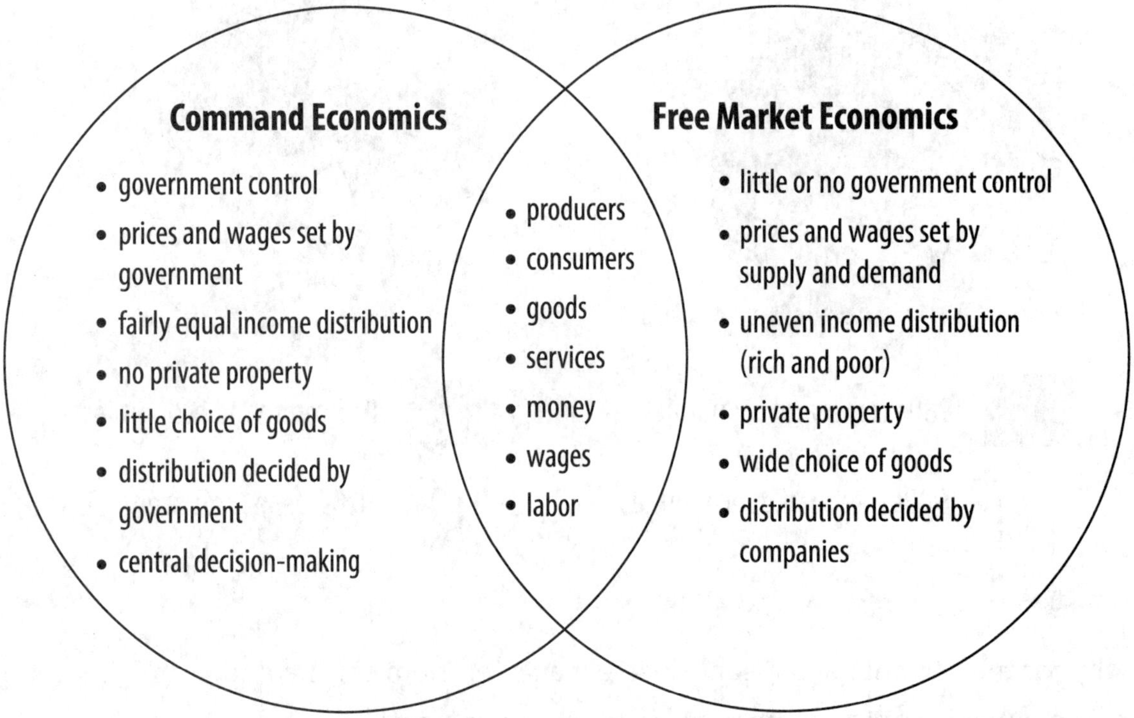

Command Economics

- government control
- prices and wages set by government
- fairly equal income distribution
- no private property
- little choice of goods
- distribution decided by government
- central decision-making

- producers
- consumers
- goods
- services
- money
- wages
- labor

Free Market Economics

- little or no government control
- prices and wages set by supply and demand
- uneven income distribution (rich and poor)
- private property
- wide choice of goods
- distribution decided by companies

1. Which system would be best for the United States? Why?

_____

_____

_____

_____

_____

_____

_____

_____

History

Name:_____ **Date:**_____

Directions: Read the text, and answer the questions.

> There are signs that people have lived in the area that is now India for many thousands of years. By about 2500 BC, they had built many cities. These had brick houses and water systems. They may have had populations of tens of thousands of people. These cities were built near river areas, where it was easy to grow crops.
>
> The people depended on agriculture. They grew crops such as wheat, rice, melons, and dates. They also grew cotton, which was spun and woven into cloth. This cloth was famous for its quality and its beauty. They also raised animals such as cattle and sheep.

1. Based on the text, what did the people of ancient India eat?
   a. wheat, rice, melons
   b. grapefruit, oranges, bananas
   c. chickens, turkeys, ducks
   d. fish, clams, lobsters

2. Based on the text, what was the cotton used for?
   a. to make animal feedbags
   b. to make tents
   c. to make beautiful cloth
   d. to make flags

3. What evidence suggests that the people of ancient India developed cities?
   a. brick houses and water systems
   b. quality cloth
   c. domesticated animals
   d. nomadic lifestyle

History

Name:_____ Date:_____

Directions: Read the text, and circle the best answer for each question.

The Indus civilization had many different communities, ranging from small towns to cities with thousands of people. Their cities were well planned. Each city had either a large fortress on one side or a wall around it. Each city had homes as well as buildings to hold grain, public baths, and businesses. They used baked brick to build their houses. They also had drainage systems, indoor bathrooms, and water supplies in the cities. Archaeologists don't know much about the religion of the people. However, they have found buildings that were probably temples.

1. Based on the text, which is the best sign of good urban planning?

   a. homes

   b. drainage systems

   c. a wall

   d. all the above

2. What does the presence of a fortress imply?

   a. They got along with each other.

   b. They had farmers.

   c. They had enemies.

   d. They wanted a big building.

3. What special buildings did they have?

   a. schools

   b. storage buildings for grain

   c. houses

   d. garages for vehicles

Name:_____ Date:_____

Directions: Look at the images, and read the questions. Circle the best answer for each.

Many artifacts like these seals carved of stone have been found. They give us clues about the Indus civilization.

1. Based on these images, what did the Indus people develop?

   a. many businesses

   b. a zoo for children

   c. writing

   d. advertising

2. How do you think these seals were made?

   a. They were painted.

   b. They were rolled.

   c. They were washed.

   d. They were carved.

3. Indus seals often showed images of animals. Some showed real animals, but others depicted imaginary creatures. What can you infer about the people who designed the seals?

   _____

   _____

   _____

Name: _____ **Date:** _____

History

Directions: Read the web, and answer the questions.

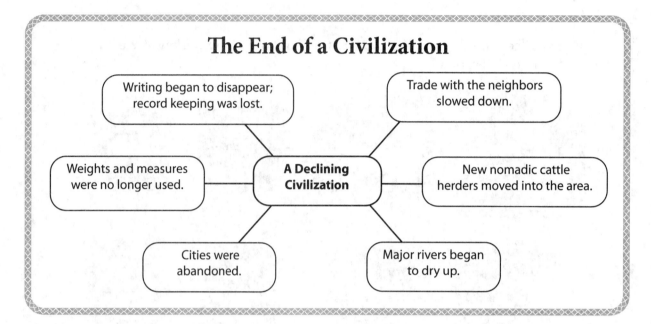

The End of a Civilization

- Writing began to disappear; record keeping was lost.
- Trade with the neighbors slowed down.
- Weights and measures were no longer used.
- **A Declining Civilization**
- New nomadic cattle herders moved into the area.
- Cities were abandoned.
- Major rivers began to dry up.

1. What change in India does this web graphic describe about the Indus civilization?

   a. grew into current-day India

   b. was taken over by other civilizations

   c. began to collapse and disappear

   d. grew into a massive civilization

2. Why does the disappearance of writing suggest that the civilization was failing?

   _____

   _____

   _____

3. Imagine you want to buy something from another person. Would you prefer to buy from someone who uses a system of weights and measures, or from someone who doesn't? Explain your answer.

   _____

   _____

   _____

Name: _____ Date: _____

Directions: Read the text, and study the images. Answer the question.

> The Indus civilization had several hundred symbols. Some scientists believe this is a language system. No one today has been able to figure it out.
>
>

1. There are many things we don't know about the Indus civilization. What might we learn if we could understand their writing?

_____

_____

_____

_____

_____

_____

_____

_____

_____

_____

Civics

Name:_____ **Date:**_____

Directions: Read the text and the questions. Then, circle the best answer for each.

In Germany, there are three branches of government. They are the executive, the legislative, and the judicial branches.

The president has little power. One of his or her main jobs is to represent the country at ceremonies. The more powerful leader is called the chancellor. He or she controls the federal government.

The executive branch is made up of the chancellor, the president, and the cabinet ministers. The chancellor serves a term of four years. If reelected, he or she can serve many terms.

The chancellor is in charge of

- government policies

- recommending who should be a cabinet minister

- deciding how many cabinet ministers there will be and what they will do

Angela Merkel, chancellor of Germany

1. Which one is true of Germany?

   a. The president is the head of state and has total power.

   b. The president can make laws independently.

   c. The president's role is ceremonial.

   d. The president is more powerful than the chancellor.

2. How long can a person remain as chancellor?

   a. only one four-year term

   b. only two four-year terms

   c. only one six-year term

   d. a long time, if reelected

3. How does the chancellor influence cabinet ministers?

   a. by suggesting which ones should be president

   b. by secretly appointing the cabinet ministers

   c. by deciding how many cabinet ministers there should be

   d. by deciding how long he/she will serve

51398—180 Days of Social Studies

Name: _____ **Date:** _____

Civics

Directions: Read the text, and study the pictures. Then, answer the questions.

The German government has been a democracy since 1990. That year, East and West Germany became one country.

Germany has a constitution called the Basic Law. It protects the people and their rights. People have the right to equality before the law. They have freedoms such as speech, assembly, news, and religion. No one can be treated badly because of their race or other reason. Because of what happened in Nazi Germany, there cannot be extreme right or left political parties any more.

The Basic Law tells how the government is to be run. There are checks and balances that make sure no one person in government has too much power. The legislative branch makes the laws. The judicial branch makes sure they are followed.

1. Which of these statements is true?

    a. Germany does not have its own constitution.

    b. The Basic Law protects the rights of people.

    c. Germany has been two countries since 1990.

    d. There are many radical political parties.

2. Which of the German rights and freedoms listed above are similar to the rights and freedoms in the United States?

    a. freedom of power, speech, and assembly

    b. the rights to extreme politics and religion

    c. freedom of news, speech, and assembly

    d. the rights to have more freedoms than others

3. How does the German constitution separate power in the government?

    a. by dividing the country in two

    b. by having the judicial branch make the laws

    c. by putting checks and balances in place

    d. by having the legislative branch make sure laws are followed

51398—180 Days of Social Studies

Name: _____ Date: _____

Directions: Read the chart, and answer the questions.

Civics

The Government of India		
Executive Branch	**Legislative Branch (Parliament)**	**Judicial Branch**
Who? • president (head of the executive, legislative, and judicial branches, and the army; elected by the legislative branch) • vice president • prime minister (runs the government) • cabinet ministers • other ministers	**Who?** • two "houses" • Council of States • House of the People	**Who?** • Supreme Court of India • high courts • district courts
What They Do • make sure the laws are passed in the country • answer to the legislative branch	**What They Do** • make or change the laws • recommend new or changed laws to the judicial branch	**What They Do** • make decisions when there are problems between the executive and the legislative branches • make judgments about laws and legal problems of the people

1. How do laws come to be in India?

   a. made by the judicial, and passed by the executive branch

   b. made by the executive, and passed by the judicial branch

   c. made by the legislative, and passed by the executive branch

   d. made by the legislative, and passed by the judicial branch

2. The power is *divided* in the Indian government. How is this done?

   _____

   _____

   _____

3. Suppose there is a conflict between the executive and the legislative branches. How can it be solved?

   _____

   _____

   _____

Name:_____ Date:_____

Directions: Read the text. Then, answer the questions.

> The constitution in India was written in 1949. It was based on the constitutions in the United States, Britain, and France. The Indian constitution guarantees six basic rights for citizens:
>
> - equality (before the law)
> - freedom of religion
> - cultural and educational rights
> - freedom
> - constitutional changes
> - no exploitation (or abuse)
>
>
> *Taj Mahal*
>
> These rights have been written to stop practices of treating people differently. Before India became independent, some people were called *untouchable*. They had few rights and had to live outside of towns. They could not enter temples or schools. The six rights are also to stop forced labor, where people have to work for no pay.

1. Which of these statements is true?

   a. The constitution in India was written in 1787.

   b. The constitution in India was based on those of Spain and Peru.

   c. The constitution in India was based on the one from Holland.

   d. The constitution in India was based on the one from the United States.

2. What rights in India are like those in our Bill of Rights? Explain.

   _____

   _____

   _____

3. India's citizens have the right to equality before the law. We have this right, too. Why do you think this right is important?

   _____

   _____

   _____

Name:_____ Date:_____

Directions: Read the text, and look at the images. Then, complete the task.

Civics

Some countries have division of power in their government. It is set out in their constitution. Three of these countries are the United States, Germany, and India.

Washington, DC

Berlin, Germany

New Delhi, India

1. Explain how these countries divide power in the government. What are the different roles that share some of the power?

_____

_____

_____

_____

_____

_____

_____

_____

_____

_____

_____

Name: _____ Date: _____

Directions: Read the text, and answer the questions.

The United States has a wide variety of geographic features. It includes arctic regions and arid deserts. It also includes wetlands and grasslands. These are shaped by geographic patterns.

Geographic patterns in the United States result mainly from geologic and atmospheric features. Geologic features make up the structure of the land. This includes the shape of landforms, water drainage, and mineral resources. Geologic features are things such as mountains and rivers.

Climate and weather are atmospheric features. This includes the sun's effects on an area. Areas in the South are warmer because of the increased effects of the sun closer to the equator.

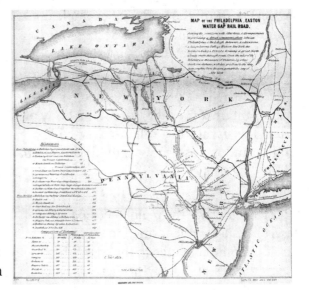

This map shows preparation for new rail lines.

1. What is an example of a geologic feature in geography?
   a. the climate
   b. mountains
   c. high winds
   d. sun's rays

2. Why does the United States feature many different geographic features?
   a. because it has deserts
   b. because of hills and valleys
   c. because it is a large country
   d. because it has a strong climate

3. What is an example of atmospheric features?
   a. weather
   b. wetlands
   c. high hills
   d. forests

Name:_____ Date:_____

Geography

Directions: Read the text, and answer the questions.

Geologic features play a key role in the physical shape of the land. For example, most mountains are formed when pieces of Earth's crust push together. They bend and fold together and form mountains.

A drainage basin—or watershed—is an area of land that provides water for a body of water. It is usually in a valley or low-lying area. Rainfall and melting snow drain down into the valley.

The Mojave Desert is an area formed by geologic features. The region became an arid desert because of the formation of the Sierra Nevada mountain range to the west. *Arid* means the desert is dry. The Sierra Nevadas stop rainfall before it gets to the Mojave Desert.

*tourist map of Death Valley,
near the Mojave Desert*

1. Which of the following are examples of the physical shape of the land?

   a. the Great Plains

   b. foot bridges

   c. City Hall

   d. the botanical gardens

2. How did the Sierra Nevadas help the Mojave Desert develop?

   a. They made the desert hilly.

   b. They made the desert cold.

   c. They made the desert dry.

   d. They made the desert wet.

3. Which statement is NOT true about a drainage basin?

   a. It is a wet area of land.

   b. It is located at a high elevation.

   c. It is a feature that helps water drain into

   d. It is usually located in a low-lying area.

Name: _____ Date: _____

Directions: Study the map, and answer the questions.

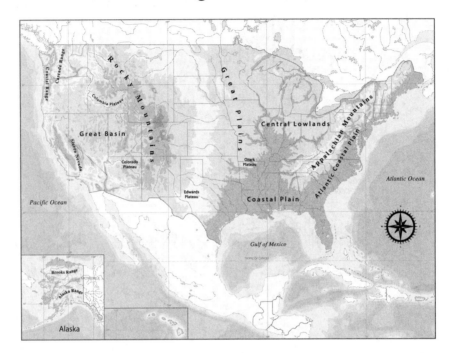

U.S. Mountain Ranges, Lowlands, and Plains

1. Which state has the highest ground?

   a. Texas   **c.** Colorado

   b. Florida   **d.** North Dakota

2. Which states are located completely in the Great Plains?

   _____

   _____

   _____

3. What features make the elevation different in the western half of the United States than it is in the eastern half?

   _____

   _____

Name: _____ Date: _____

Geography

Directions: Read the text, and study the graphic. Answer the questions.

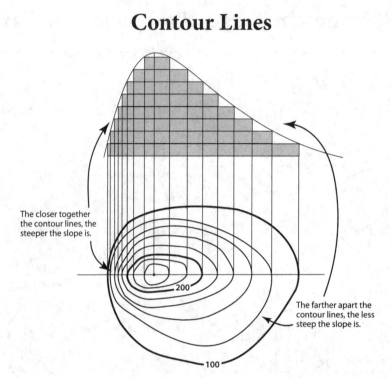

Contour Lines

The closer together the contour lines, the steeper the slope is.

200

The farther apart the contour lines, the less steep the slope is.

100

Topographical maps often use contour lines to show the shape of the land. If lines are far apart, the area is flatter, such as a field or plain. If the lines are closer together, they show a hill or a valley. Contour lines also show if the slope of the hill is steep or gentle.

1. Why do people use topographical maps with contour lines? Circle all that apply.

   a. to see where people are   **c.** to understand the weather

   b. to see hills and valleys   **d.** to picture the color of the land

2. If you were to draw a large, flat meadow, what would the contour lines look like?

   a. very close together

   b. far apart

   c. some lines close and some lines far apart

   d. no lines are needed in a flat area

3. What kind of topography does your city or town have? Is it hilly, flat, or both?

   _____

   _____

51398—180 Days of Social Studies

Name:_____ Date:_____

Directions: Think about contour maps that have closer lines showing steeper slopes and lines farther apart showing flat or shallow slopes. Fill in the bottom map with contour lines. Mark the oceans, the Rocky and Appalachian Mountains, and the plains in the central United States.

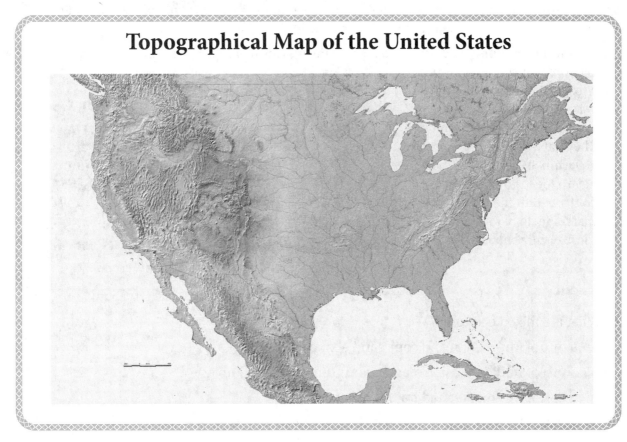

Topographical Map of the United States

Economics

Name: _____ Date: _____

Directions: Read the text, and answer the questions.

There are three kinds of economies: traditional, command, and market. Traditional economy is based on hunting, gathering, farming, or fishing. This type of economy can still be found in a few isolated places in the world.

Most economies today are mixed economies. This means they use different parts of the three types of economies. Mixed economies can look very different. Some of them are mostly market economies. They have only a little government control. Others have a lot of government control. But, they have some market factors, too. Some are more evenly balanced.

Subsistence farming is part of a traditional economy.

1. What is a mixed economy?
   a. a mix of free market and command economies
   b. a mix of traditional, free market, and command economies
   c. a mix of free market and traditional economies
   d. a mix of traditional and command economies

2. Why do most countries today have mixed economies?
   a. People can't decide which is better.
   b. Traditional economies are confusing.
   c. Each type of economy has important benefits.
   d. Mixed economies give the government control.

3. Why aren't all mixed economies the same?

   _____

   _____

   _____

Name: _____ Date: _____

Directions: Read the text, and answer the questions.

Countries make choices that help meet people's needs and wants. These choices lead to the type of economy in that country. Each economy has to answer three basic questions: (1) What is produced? (2) How is it produced and distributed? (3) For whom is it produced?

In a command economy, the government decides how much of each good is produced. It decides where and how the goods are produced. It decides how the goods get to the consumers. It decides which consumers get them.

In a market economy, supply and demand lead to decisions about how much to produce and when to purchase. Availability and price decide who will buy and who will not. In a mixed economy, companies or individuals make many of these decisions about goods. The government often makes decisions about services such as police protection and education.

Economics

1. Who or what decides the three basic questions in a mixed economy?
   a. the central government
   b. the business owners
   c. the companies or individuals
   d. the consumers of the goods and services

2. Why does the government often make decisions about providing certain services, such as police?
   a. to make sure everyone can have the service no matter who they are
   b. to make sure there are some police in the community
   c. to reduce the need for private security businesses
   d. to have a way to spend taxes that have been collected

3. Who likely runs small businesses in a mixed economy?
   a. the federal government
   b. individuals or small companies
   c. the local government
   d. multinational corporations

Name: _____ Date:_____

Directions: Study the graphic, and answer the questions.

Economics

Types of Economies

Command Economy
- military, police, fire
- foreign trade
- infrastructure
- social programs
- may control significant natural resources

Traditional Economy
- hunting for food
- subsistence fishing
- impact of traditions such as Christmas and Thanksgiving
- traditional communities following old ways

Market Economy
- private property
- law of supply and demand to determine production
- law of supply and demand to determine wages and prices
- self-interest/profit motive
- innovation
- privately funded education and health care

Mixed Economy

1. How does Christmas affect a mixed economy in a country like the United States? Circle the two best answers.

   a. Producers arrange to have large numbers of goods available for the season.

   b. People save their money so they do not have any left to purchase goods.

   c. It has little impact because people buy goods and services all year long.

   d. Producers need to have breaks after Christmas to restock.

2. Government control of social programs varies from country to country. Explain which social programs you think the government should run.

   _____

   _____

   _____

3. Why is it helpful for highways and railroad lines to be managed by the government?

   _____

   _____

51398—180 Days of Social Studies

© *Shell Education*

Name: _____ **Date:** _____

Directions: Study the graphic, and answer the questions.

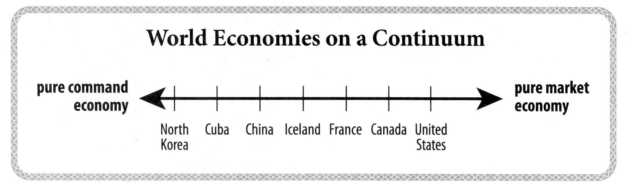

World Economies on a Continuum

pure command economy ← — — — — — — — → pure market economy

North Korea   Cuba   China   Iceland   France   Canada   United States

1. Which countries have significant government control of the economy?

   a. United States

   b. North Korea

   c. Canada

   d. France

2. Why isn't the United States located right at the pure market economy end of the continuum?

   _____

   _____

   _____

   _____

3. A new country has a lot of private industry. The government controls a few industries. Parents pay for school and health care. There is no welfare or social security. Explain where this country would be placed on the continuum.

   _____

   _____

   _____

   _____

   _____

Economics

Name: _____   Date: _____

Directions: Read the text, and answer the question.

The founding fathers made sure that the Constitution protected many elements of a free market, such as the right to own private property. At the same time, they wrote that the federal government should "promote the general welfare."

1. Imagine you were a founder of a new nation. What kind of economy would you establish? Why?

_____

_____

_____

_____

_____

_____

_____

Name:_____ Date:_____

Directions: Read the text, and answer the questions.

China is one of the world's oldest civilizations. The Huang He, or Yellow River, area was settled by 3000 BC. Chinese history is often divided into dynasties. A dynasty is a series of rulers from the same family. Some dynasties lasted for hundreds of years. Others lasted for only short time periods.

Many important religions and ethical ideas developed in China. Confucius shared ideas of how to live. Daoism states that people should live in harmony with nature. They believe that a whole is made of connected opposites. This is called yin and yang.

Buddhism is based on the ideas of the Buddha. Buddhists believe that all actions have consequences. Any actions you take now will affect your future. Bad actions lead to bad times in the future.

yin and yang symbol

1. Why did some dynasties last only a short time?
   a. The rulers didn't like the job.
   b. Another family took control.
   c. They ran out of ideas.
   d. Their turn ended.

2. Why do Buddhists think you should try to do good?
   a. To live in harmony with nature.
   b. You are more popular if you are kind.
   c. Good things will happen to you in the future.
   d. Bad people end up in jail.

3. Which could be part of the yin and yang concept?
   a. basketball and baseball
   b. blue and yellow
   c. old and young
   d. apple and pear

History

Name:_____ Date:_____

Directions: Read the text, and answer the questions.

Qin Shi Huang was the first emperor of China. Over 2,200 years ago, he brought together all the warring states to form the Chinese empire. He built himself an incredible tomb. He was buried with over 8,000 life-sized terra-cotta (clay) warriors. Every warrior was unique. They were carefully molded and shaped to have different faces, hands, weapons, and uniforms. Each statue had many details. There were even treads on the shoes of kneeling warriors.

Thousands of people worked to create the statues. Different body parts were made by different workers and then attached together. Each statue was given its own special look. Then they were painted and covered with lacquer.

terra-cotta warriors

1. What is unique about the terra cotta warriors?
   a. They had the same face.
   b. They were each different.
   c. They could move to new places.
   d. They all carried weapons.

2. Why do you think Qin Shi Huang built his tomb?
   a. He lived in the tomb before he died.
   b. He wanted to be remembered after he died.
   c. He wanted servants and warriors to die with him.
   d. He wanted work for his people.

3. Why did they make each figure unique?

   _____

   _____

   _____

Name:_____ Date:_____

Directions: Study the web, and answer the questions.

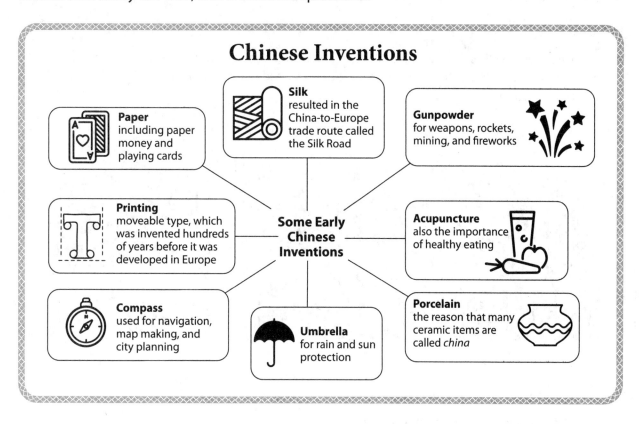

1. Umbrellas were used to protect people from the sun. Which people probably had the lightest skin?

   a. enslaved people

   b. nobles and royalty

   c. common people

   d. farmers

2. Why was gunpowder an important invention?

   _____

   _____

3. The Chinese would not tell other people how they made silk. Why do you think they kept the process a secret for as long as possible?

   _____

   _____

   _____

History

Name:_____ Date:_____

Directions: Look at the images, and answer the questions.

The Great Wall of China was built to protect the country from invasions. It stretches over 5,500 miles. Because it is so long, it took hundreds of years to build. It is a famous symbol of China.

1. Why was the wall built over many hundreds of years?

   a. It was too long to build in a short period of time.

   b. They needed new sections at different times.

   c. Parts were damaged.

   d. There was not enough rock to build it.

2. What features in the images show how the wall was guarded?

   _____

   _____

   _____

3. What famous symbols represent the United States today?

   _____

   _____

   _____

Name: _____ Date:_____

Directions: Read the chart. Fill in the United States Today column.

Ancient China and United States Today	
Ancient China	**United States Today**
Agriculture • Most people were farmers. • They had hard lives. • Most work was done by hand. • Farms were owned by the nobles; they let people work on small family-run farms. • Farmers gave the government some of their crops.	**Agriculture**
Life in the Cities • There were many jobs in the cities, such as shop keepers, artists, and craftspeople, government officials, scholars. • People studied for exams to get government jobs.	**Life in the Cities**
Family Life • The father was in charge. • The wife and children had to obey the father. • Women took care of the house and children. • Parents decided who their children would marry. • Only rich boys went to school.	**Family Life**
Government • The head was the emperor. For many years, people believed the emperor was blessed by heaven. • Government officials were appointed by the emperor (or his officials). • Some officials were family members. • Some officials were nobles. • Some officials took exams to get a job. • Some officials belonged to wealthy, important families.	**Government**

Name: _____   Date: _____

Directions: Read the text and questions. Then, circle the best answer.

Civics

> We are Americans. We share the values of freedom, liberty, equality, and justice. These are democratic values. We believe that people should live in a society with freedoms and rights for all people. The rule of law keeps order, protects our rights, and limits the power of government.
>
> Our ideas about democracy developed over time. They came about at a great cost for many people. In the 1700s, Britain passed laws for America. These laws took away rights of the colonists. The American leaders had tried to tell the British that they wanted a say in the way they were governed. But the British king and government would not listen. So the American leaders decided it was time to make a big change—a revolution.

1. What does it mean to have democratic values?

   a. Our society and government should tell us what to do and say.

   b. Our society and government should make us live by their values.

   c. Our society and government should make us follow one specific religion.

   d. Our society and government should allow us human rights and freedoms.

2. In a democracy, why is it important to have a government set laws and keep order?

   a. Without laws and order, a monarch would not be able to control a country.

   b. If there were no laws or order, we could do whatever we want to do.

   c. Without laws and order, citizen rights would not be protected.

   d. If there were no laws or order, a tyrant would not be able to control a country.

3. Why did American leaders finally decide to make a big change? Which one is NOT true?

   a. The British government took rights away from the colonists.

   b. The British government allowed Americans to have a say in the way they were governed.

   c. The British government refused to pass laws for American colonists.

   d. The British government would not listen to the colonists.

51398—180 Days of Social Studies

Name: _____ Date: _____

Directions: Read the text, and answer the questions.

Thomas Jefferson wrote the Declaration of Independence. He used the words "life, liberty and the pursuit of happiness." These were John Locke's ideas. He was a philosopher, or a thinker, from Britain in the 1600s. He wrote about the natural rights of all people. These same ideas soon led to a revolution in France. At about the same time, they helped declare a revolution in America.

In 1776, the members of the Continental Congress shared the Declaration of Independence. They declared a new government. They stated that the people would be free from Britain. It was dangerous to write and sign it. Some signers were caught by the British and put to death as traitors. Some had their houses burned. Some fought in the war. They risked their lives so Americans would be free.

Thomas Jefferson

Civics

1. Which of these is true about Thomas Jefferson?

   a. He first thought up the ideas of life, liberty, and the pursuit of happiness.

   b. He first wrote about the natural rights of people.

   c. He was a philosopher from the 1600s.

   d. He used Locke's ideas when he was writing.

2. People thought about the words of philosophers. They wrote them in documents. What other impact did their ideas have in the United States and France?

   a. They helped the Americans and the French get along with the British.

   b. They helped the Americans and the French get along better with each other.

   c. They helped the Americans and the French decide to fight for their freedom.

   d. They made the Americans and the French fight against each other.

3. How did working for democracy cost many people?

   a. They had to pay money to buy democracy for the country.

   b. They had to give up natural resources to get democracy.

   c. They had to give up their lives and homes for democracy.

   d. They had to work long hours in factories to get democracy.

Civics

Name: _____ Date: _____

Directions: Look at the chart, and answer the questions.

Rights, Responsibilities, and Roles from the Constitution		
Rights to…	**Responsibilities to…**	**Roles—You Could…**
• freedom of religion, speech, press, assembly, and petition • bear arms • protection from search and seizure • life, liberty, pursuit of happiness • own property • fair, speedy trial • citizenship • work • vote • run for an elected office	• support the Constitution • stay up to date on issues • respect others, their rights, and their beliefs • be part of your community; go to community meetings • volunteer; be part of the common good • vote and be part of the democratic process • obey all laws • pay taxes • serve on a jury • defend your country	• be the president • join the military • join the Peace Corps • work to help others • work for the federal, state, or local government • do another job of your choice

1. What rights do citizens have in this country?

    a. They have freedom of religion, speech, press, assembly, and petition.

    b. They have the right to have a smart phone.

    c. They have the right to pay taxes.

    d. They have the right to join the military.

2. What responsibilities do citizens have in this country?

    _____

    _____

3. What citizen roles can children in this country take on?

    _____

    _____

51398—180 Days of Social Studies

Name:_____ Date:_____

Directions: Read the text, and study the pictures. Then, answer the questions.

All through the history of our country, new citizens have always been important to our democracy.

There are many benefits to becoming a citizen of our country. Adult citizens can vote and have a say in how the government runs our country. They gain many rights and freedoms that they may not have had in their old countries. They have the right to work hard, achieve, and earn success. They are not held back by their age, race, gender, or religion.

Newcomers also accept the responsibilities of citizens. They follow laws and support their communities. They bring and share their ideas, talents, and traditions. They volunteer and help others. They promote the common good for all.

1. Which is a benefit to becoming a citizen?

   a. American citizens have many rights and freedoms.

   b. Citizens must go to baseball games.

   c. All Americans are immigrants or come from families of immigrants.

   d. Newcomers play an important role in the country.

2. Imagine you are growing up in a country like North Korea or China. Why might you want to come live in the United States?

   _____

   _____

3. What things do you do in your community to promote the common good?

   _____

   _____

   _____

Civics

Name: _____ Date: _____

Directions: Read the question. Then, complete the task.

voting

immigration to United States

1. What do you know about each of these:

   a. American values

   _____

   _____

   _____

   _____

   b. Rights, responsibilities, and roles of being a citizen

   _____

   _____

   _____

   _____

   c. Citizenship and immigration

   _____

   _____

   _____

   _____

Name:_____ Date:_____

Directions: Read the text, and answer the questions.

Geography

China has one of the oldest civilizations in the world. Its history is 7,000 years old. Chinese civilization began along the Yellow River, close to present day Xi'an. For hundreds of years, China was quite isolated from the rest of the world. Deserts, mountains, and oceans shielded China from most invaders. Little of the Chinese culture spread beyond these natural borders.

The Chinese thought they lived in the middle of the world, because they were surrrounded by natural barriers. They called themselves the Middle Kingdom. Over time, China's land area and population grew. It expanded south past the Yangtze River. It embraced the eastern seashores. It reached to the far west past the Turfan Depression. It stretched north into the Gobi Desert.

1. What is a barrier?
   a. a passageway leading to a new discovery
   b. an obstacle preventing access
   c. the outer part of a region
   d. the middle location of a region

2. Based on the text, how did living in isolation influence Chinese beliefs?
   a. They believed they had no enemies.
   b. They believed they lived in the middle of the world.
   c. They believed they must share their culture.
   d. They believed invaders would change their culture.

3. What geographical features can prevent different societies from connecting?
   a. languages
   b. rough terrain
   c. extreme temperatures
   d. pollution

Geography

Name:_____ Date:_____

Directions: Read the text, and answer the questions.

Chinese civilization began along the banks of the Yellow River. This river flows from the western Tibetan plateau to the northeast coast of China. As the river flowed, it collected yellow silt. It also left deposits of silt. These deposits formed barriers. In time, the river changed its pathway, flowing around the barriers. The unpredictable river's path caused flooding. It destroyed villages. It also replenished the soil with fertile silt.

People grew crops and kept pigs and dogs. Several groups worked together to solve the problem of the Yellow River's floods. Canals were built to redistribute the water.

aerial view of Yellow River, China

1. Why might the Yellow River have been called the River of Tears?
   a. Many wars were fought at this river.
   c. Floods destroyed villages.
   b. It is a treacherous river to travel.
   d. Building canals is hard work.

2. Why did people settle along the Yellow River?
   a. It provided water, transportation, and fertile land.
   b. It flowed around their villages.
   c. It was easy to build canals to redistribute flood waters.
   d. Silt barriers created lakes where they could fish.

3. Water follows the path of least resistance. Use this idea to explain why the Yellow River changed its course.

   _____

   _____

   _____

Name: _____ Date: _____

Directions: Study the map, and answer the questions.

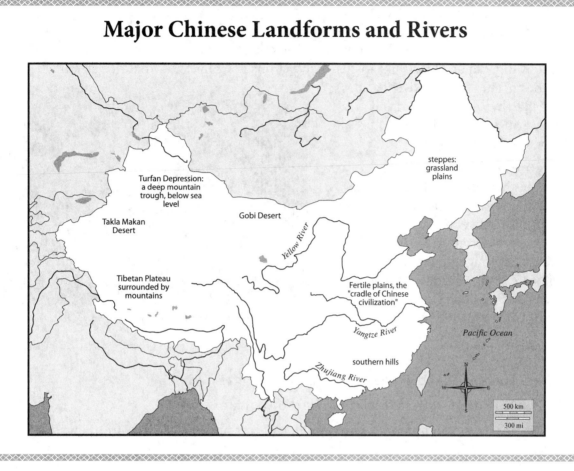

Major Chinese Landforms and Rivers

Turfan Depression: a deep mountain trough, below sea level

Takla Makan Desert

Gobi Desert

steppes: grassland plains

Yellow River

Tibetan Plateau surrounded by mountains

Fertile plains, the "cradle of Chinese civilization"

Yangtze River

Pacific Ocean

southern hills

Zhujiang River

500 km

300 mi

1. In what direction are the Fertile Plains from the Turfan Depression?

   a. southeast   **c.** east

   b. northeast   **d.** west

2. In what direction are the Fertile Plains from the Tibetan Plateau?

   a. north   **c.** northeast

   b. east   **d.** southeast

3. The land route of the Silk Road trade went in an east-west direction. What were some of the challenges found along this route?

_____

_____

_____

Name: _____   Date: _____

Geography

Directions: Read the text, and answer the questions.

The Yangtze River is the longest river in China. Silt that was carried and collected along its journey fertilized the lands on either side of the river. Archaeologists study the past by digging up objects like fossils. Excavations in China show that rice farming began in the ancient Yangtze River basin. The marshy and hilly lands and the warm and humid temperatures supported rice farming.

Rice farming was hard work. Farm families had many children to help with the work. Simple houses on stilts were built above the wet fields. China's culture grew from an agricultural base. Wars were fought for control of this valuable land. Alliances were formed. Dynasties rose and fell as China's boundaries expanded.

terraced rice crop in China

1. Why did people fight over the lands of eastern China?

    a. The land was fertile, so food could be grown there.

    b. The land was mountainous and provided secret passages to hide from invaders.

    c. It was next to the sea, so people could fish.

    d. The river systems provided water.

2. What is an archaeological excavation?

    a. a site with remains from earlier civilizations

    b. a site where food is grown

    c. a graveyard

    d. a site studied

3. Why did rice farmers build houses on stilts? What special features does your house have because of geographical challenges in your area?

    _____

    _____

    _____

51398—180 Days of Social Studies   © Shell Education

Name:_____ Date:_____

Directions: Read the text, and answer the questions.

Ancient China was a mysterious place to the outside world because of its natural barriers. Chinese inventions such as weapons, tools, silks, and pottery brought traders to the region. This strengthened China's economy. In time, trade routes opened, and people traveled through China's natural borders.

Geographical differences split the country into north and south regions. The north looked west across deserts and narrow mountain passes for trade. Mules and carts carried goods in the cool, dry climate. The south's wet, monsoon climate allowed for river travel. Merchants in the south also used treacherous mountain passes to reach southern Asia. In time, north and south sea ports opened.

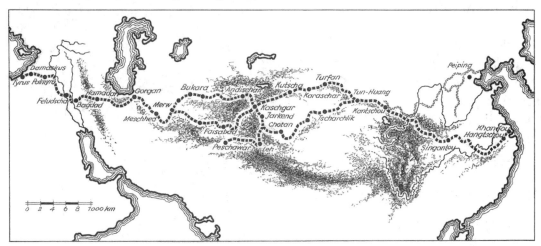

old map of the Silk Road trading route through China

1. Why do you think China was a mysterious place to the outside world?

_____

_____

_____

_____

_____

_____

_____

Name: _____ Date: _____

Economics

Directions: Read the text, and answer the questions.

Production is the creation of goods and services. Production turns materials into the goods that people want or need. Production can also turn knowledge and ideas into goods and services.

Four factors affect production: land, capital, labor, and enterprise. Land includes actual land. It also means the resources that come from the land. Capital is the money a company uses to purchase resources. It also includes property like buildings or vehicles. Labor is the activity of humans. They convert resources into goods or provide a service. The last factor is enterprise. Entrepreneurs manage the businesses. They make decisions and take the risk of losing capital if they are wrong.

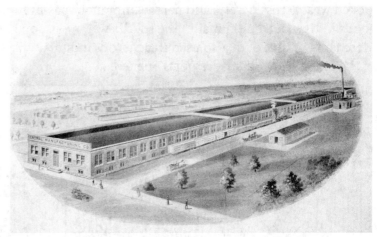

a manufacturing company in 1906

1. What do entrepreneurs risk?
   a. making decisions
   b. losing money
   c. the four factors of production
   d. converting resources into goods

2. What is capital?
   a. money for a business
   b. the business managers
   c. farm fields
   d. the captain of a fishing boat

3. What is production?
   a. running a business to make a profit
   b. collecting more capital
   c. creating the goods and services people want or need
   d. deciding what should be created and when to do it

Name: _____ **Date:** _____

Directions: Read the text, and answer the questions.

Capital can be the tools, machines, and buildings that are needed to produce a product. These are physical items that can be bought or leased. They can wear out. They may need to be replaced. Some companies prefer to lease rather than buy. They may not be able to pay the whole price for a new product.

The capital in a factory is the machinery. The building is also a form of capital. A fishing business's capital includes boats or ships, nets, and other gear. A farming business has barns, tractors, combines, and other equipment. Capital can be used to buy a factory building or a fishing boat.

Capital can also be the money used to buy land. Land is an asset. But land is not actual capital.

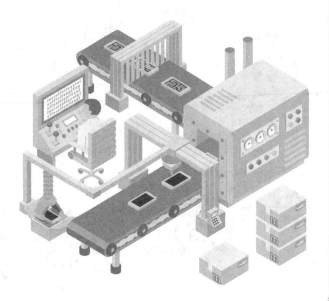

1. Based on the text, what can capital be used for?
   a. to buy lunch for all the workers
   b. to buy physical items like a harvester
   c. to bill customers for products they purchase
   d. to make decisions about what should be produced

2. Why do companies sometimes lease physical items?
   a. Leasing is a service that companies appreciate.
   b. The company wants to use the equipment.
   c. The company can try different kinds.
   d. The company can't afford to pay the whole price at once.

3. Which of the following is NOT capital?
   a. money
   b. land
   c. a silo
   d. a computer

Name:_____ Date:_____

Economics

Directions: Study the images, and answer the questions.

Land—Any Natural Resource Used in Production

Fish are found in the water. Water and fish are considered land.

Highways or structures can be built on soil or rock. Soil and rock are considered land.

Rainforests and hardwood forests are considered land.

Materials like coal are taken from the earth, so they are considered land.

Farms where crops can be planted and grown are considered land.

Oceans, rivers, and lakes are considered land.

1. Why are oil and coal considered to be land?

   a. They are needed by producers.

   b. They are black like rich soil.

   c. They are resources that come from the earth.

   d. They are resources that are nonrenewable.

2. Why are oceans and fish considered to be land?

   _____

   _____

3. The total land on Earth is fairly stable, but resources can change. Which images on this page could decrease and may not be replaced? Why?

   _____

   _____

   _____

51398—180 Days of Social Studies

Name: _____ Date: _____

Directions: Look at the photos, and answer the questions.

An entrepreneur wants to provide a new service.

Workers are needed to produce goods and services.

Economics

1. Which of the following is not an example of labor to produce goods and services?

   a. chef

   b. parent

   c. factory worker

   d. garbage collector

2. Enterprise requires the entrepreneur to take risks and make decisions in business. What are some risks for a new business?

   _____

   _____

   _____

   _____

3. Think of your own interests and talents. What type of labor or enterprise interests you? Why?

   _____

   _____

   _____

   _____

Name: _____ Date: _____

Directions: Study the image, and answer the question.

1. Explain how each of the four factors that affect production is represented in the image.

_____

_____

_____

_____

_____

_____

_____

_____

Name:_____ **Date:**_____

Directions: Read the text, and answer the questions.

Two brothers founded Rome about 750 BC. Kings ruled it for many years. Then a group of citizens threw out the king. Rome became a republic. The Roman Republic grew into a huge and powerful empire. At first, the power was held by only a small group of citizens.

Then, over time, power shifted until a system of three-part government developed. The three branches were the consuls, the senate, and the assemblies. Eventually, they also had an emperor. There was a system of checks and balances to make sure no branch had too much power.

Roman Senate

1. Who founded the Roman Republic?

  a. a single king   **c.** a small group of citizens

  b. two brothers   **d.** an emperor

2. What is the purpose of checks and balances?

  a. No one is king.   **c.** No one makes bad laws.

  b. No one has too much power.   **d.** No one is a leader.

3. What were the three parts of the Roman government?

  a. the House of Representatives

  b. the consuls

  c. the senate

  d. the assemblies

Name: _____ Date: _____

History

Directions: Read the text, and answer the questions.

Slavery is a system in which some people own others as property. Rome had many enslaved people. Some were captured in wars. Some were sold into slavery. Others were born to slavery.

Gladiators were slaves who fought animals or each other in places called circuses. They often fought until they were killed. The common citizens of Rome were called *plebeians*. They were free and had rights. Over time, they gained more power in the government. The powerful, wealthy aristocrats were called the *patricians*. Free noncitizens from different parts of the empire were known as *aliens*.

1. Based on the text, why were there many enslaved people in ancient Rome?

   a. People were captured and enslaved during wars.

   b. People were born to slavery.

   c. People were sold into slavery.

   d. all the above

2. Who were the "aliens" in Rome?

   a. gladiators of Rome

   b. free noncitizens of Rome

   c. enslaved people from outside Rome

   d. wealthy aristocrats from Rome

3. The government didn't want the plebeians to form mobs and fight them. They gave the plebeians enough food and entertainment to keep them happy. What Roman expression do you think describes this idea?

   a. food and fun

   b. let them eat cake

   c. keep them quiet

   d. bread and circuses

51398—180 Days of Social Studies

© *Shell Education*

Name: _____   Date: _____

Directions: Study the map, and answer the questions.

History

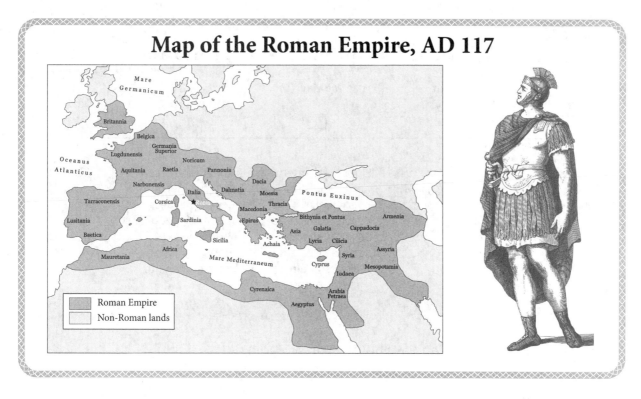

Map of the Roman Empire, AD 117

1. Where did the empire focus most of its growth?

   a. around the Atlantic Ocean (Oceanus Atlanticus)

   b. around the German Sea (Mare Germanicum)

   c. around the Mediterranean Sea (Mare Mediterraneum)

   d. around Africa and the the Black Sea (Pontus Euxinus)

2. Soldiers could march about 20 miles every day. What other qualities would someone need to be a good soldier?

   _____

   _____

3. The Romans sent citizens to live in each area they took over. Why would that help the new area become part of the empire?

   _____

   _____

   _____

History

Name:_____ **Date:**_____

Directions: Look at the timeline, and answer the questions.

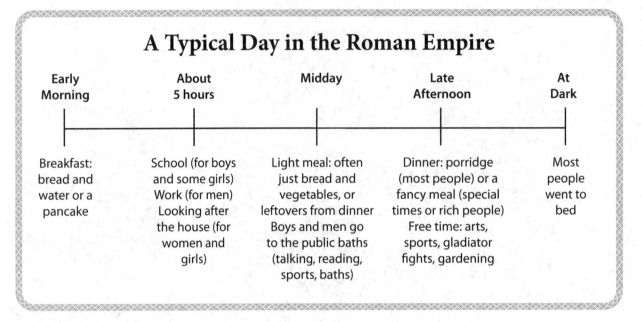

A Typical Day in the Roman Empire

Early Morning	About 5 hours	Midday	Late Afternoon	At Dark
Breakfast: bread and water or a pancake	School (for boys and some girls) Work (for men) Looking after the house (for women and girls)	Light meal: often just bread and vegetables, or leftovers from dinner Boys and men go to the public baths (talking, reading, sports, baths)	Dinner: porridge (most people) or a fancy meal (special times or rich people) Free time: arts, sports, gladiator fights, gardening	Most people went to bed

1. Where did Roman men spend five hours each day?

   a. at work

   b. at recreational activities

   c. at the shops

   d. at the religious temple

2. What are similarities between a Roman child's life and your life?

   _____

   _____

   _____

   _____

3. What are differences between a Roman child's life and your life?

   _____

   _____

   _____

   _____

History

Name: _____ **Date:** _____

Directions: Study the web, and answer the question.

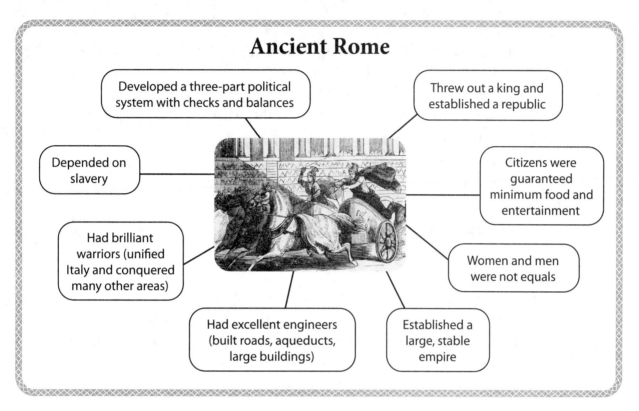

Ancient Rome

Developed a three-part political system with checks and balances

Threw out a king and established a republic

Depended on slavery

Citizens were guaranteed minimum food and entertainment

Had brilliant warriors (unified Italy and conquered many other areas)

Women and men were not equals

Had excellent engineers (built roads, aqueducts, large buildings)

Established a large, stable empire

1. Use a Venn diagram to compare ancient Rome and the modern United States.

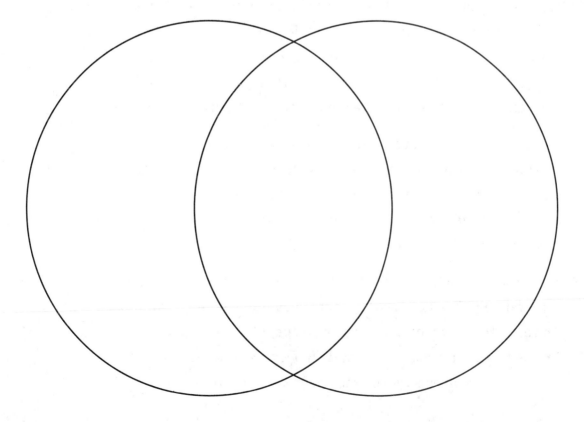

Civics

Name: _____ **Date:** _____

Directions: Read the text and questions. Then, circle all answers that are correct.

> Our Constitution has served as a model for other countries. When other countries were writing their constitutions, they looked at ours for ideas. They looked at how we divided power in our government. They looked at our freedoms and rights.
>
> The Mexican Constitution was inspired by ours. Their citizens have the right to
>
> - freedom of expression (press, speech, petition, assembly)
> - bear arms (very limited over the years)
> - vote in elections
> - be elected
> - health care paid for by the government
> - education for all
> - a job and housing
> - freedom of religion
>
> The rights of citizens are written in the Mexican constitution. But they are not always respected. There have been many reports of cruelty toward the people. These are described by human rights agencies and in the news.

1. The Mexican constitution was inspired by the American document. But some rights are different. Which of these is not a right for citizens of the United States?

   a. the freedom of press, speech, petition, and assembly

   b. the freedom to vote in an election or to be elected to government

   c. the freedom of education for all people in the country

   d. the right to government paid health care for all citizens

2. Do all citizens of Mexico have the same rights and freedoms?

   a. All citizens have the right to vote and to be elected.

   b. Only some citizens have the right to vote and to be elected.

   c. Only some citizens have the right to an education.

   d. Only some citizens have the right to health care.

3. How do we know that the rights and freedoms of citizens of Mexico are not always respected?

   a. The rights and freedoms of citizens are not written in the constitution.

   b. The government writes reports to tell the people.

   c. The news agencies study and report on people's rights.

   d. There are no problems with citizens' rights and freedoms.

Name: _____ **Date:** _____

Directions: Read the text. Then, circle all answers that are correct.

> In Mexico, the government controls many things. It is in charge of the economy. It owns all natural resources, including oil and gas, in the country. It controls most of the electricity, too. It decides on the size of farms. Many people are poor in this country and have only farm crops to live on.
>
> The citizens have responsibilities to their country. They pay taxes. They must enlist in the Mexican army or the National Guard.
>
> Citizens who were not born in Mexico do not have all the same rights as those who were. They cannot be police officers or pilots. They cannot become government officials.

1. Some things are the same and different between Mexico's government and ours. Which of these are true?

   a. In Mexico and our country, the government controls all natural resources.

   b. In Mexico and in our country, the government has a constitution.

   c. In Mexico and in our country, the government controls the electricity.

   d. In Mexico and in our country, the government is in charge of the economy.

2. Which of these are citizen responsibilities in Mexico?

   a. They must pay for their education and health care.

   b. They must pay taxes to the government.

   c. They must serve the Peace Corps.

   d. They must serve as police officers or pilots.

3. Some citizens are not born in Mexico. How are they treated differently from those who are born in the country?

   a. They do not have freedom of speech or religion.

   b. They do not have access to education or health care.

   c. They cannot work in the army or the National Guard.

   d. They cannot become government officials.

Civics

Name:_____ Date:_____

Directions: Study the chart, and answer the questions.

The United States and the Philippines				
April to August 1898	**1899–1902**	**1902–1946**	**1935–1973**	**February 1987**
Spanish-American War The United States won the war. As a result, we controlled the Philippines.	Philippine-American War The United States won this war.	The United States set up a democratic government. We helped them with education. We trained their teachers. We taught English in the schools.	1945: end of World War II 1946: The Philippines got full independence. Constitutions were written and changed.	The final version of the constitution was accepted. It has a bill of rights. It lists citizen rights and freedoms. It says how the government is run.

1. How did the United States become involved in the government of the Philippines?

   a. The United States asked if they could help them write their constitution.

   b. The Philippines became one of the states in America.

   c. The United States controlled the Philippines after winning a war.

   d. The United States bought the Philippines from Mexico.

2. When did the Philippines get full independence from the United States?

   a. after they had a final version of their constitution

   b. after they had set up schools in the country

   c. after World War II

   d. after the Spanish-American war

3. Pretend you lived in the Philippines in the early 1900s. What things would you have enjoyed that came from the United States? Why?

   _____

   _____

   _____

Name: _____   **Date:** _____

Directions: Read the text, and study the pictures. Then, answer the questions.

Civics

Philippine Citizen Rights and Duties	
Philippine Citizen Rights	**Philippine Citizen Duties**
Rights to • life, liberty, property • freedom of expression (speech, press, assembly, petition, beliefs) • due process, silence, legal counsel, speedy trial • privacy; no searches and seizures • freedom of religion • travel • vote	There is no article on citizen duties in the constitution. But there are separate laws that tell citizens they must pay taxes. The constitution says that schools will teach children: • patriotism • respect for human rights • respect for national heroes • the rights and duties of citizens • good values • self-discipline • thinking skills

1. Which of these is true about Filipino citizens?

    a. They have the right to due process and a speedy trial.

    b. They do not have to pay taxes.

    c. They must have self-discipline.

    d. They do not have the right to privacy and freedom of religion.

2. Pretend you are a citizen of the Philippines. How are your rights and freedoms the same or different from those in our country?

    _____

    _____

3. What things do Filipino schools teach that are the same as what you learn in your school?

    _____

    _____

Name:_____ **Date:**_____

Civics

Directions: The constitutions in some countries were inspired by ours. Two of these countries are Mexico and the Philippines. Fill in two of the three columns by listing the rights and responsibilities of citizens.

Citizen Rights and Responsibilities		
United States	**Mexico**	**Philippines**

51398—*180 Days of Social Studies*

Name:_____ **Date:**_____

Directions: Read the text, and answer the questions.

Human activity has a direct impact on the environment. Pollution is one way that people affect Earth. Pollution happens when something makes the air, ground, or water dirty in some way.

Another impact humans have on the planet is through overpopulation. There are more people on the planet, and they are living longer. This means more people are affecting the environment, food needs, and housing.

People leave *footprints* on Earth. A carbon footprint is the amount of gases, such as carbon dioxide, that people release into the air. This can be done through transportation, such as cars and buses, or from heating buildings and homes.

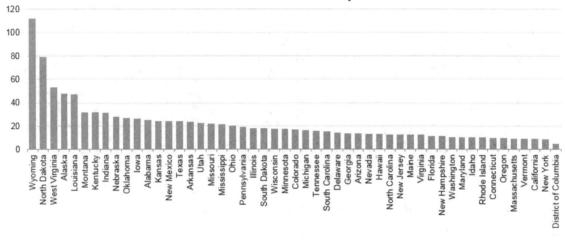

Per Person Carbon Emissions by State, 2014

1. Which of the following is an example of ground pollution?

   a. a boat with leaking gas

   b. car fumes in the air

   c. dropping garbage on the ground

   d. using your air conditioner on high

2. What is something that contributes to the human carbon footprint?

   a. walking to school

   b. heating homes

   c. going camping

   d. riding a bike

3. How does overpopulation affect the planet? Circle all that apply.

   a. More people means more housing needs.

   b. More people means more food produced.

   c. More people means more garden plants.

   d. More people means less cars on the road.

Geography

Name: _____ Date: _____

Directions: Read the chart, and answer the questions.

Examples of Pollution and Its Effects				
Air	**Ground**	**Water**	**Noise**	**Light**
Cars, buses, planes, and other vehicles release gases and fumes into the air, making it dirty.	People litter. They drop garbage and leave it on the ground.	Human garbage, such as plastic bottles, accumulates in the oceans.	Noise caused by machines and vehicles may force wildlife to find new areas to live.	Really bright lights can change the natural cycles of animals. They may think it's day when it's night.

1. What is an example of light pollution effects?

    a. Garbage accumulates on the ground.

    b. Fumes cause the sky to get smoggy.

    c. Animals get confused about the time.

    d. Animals get less food to eat.

2. What is a way that both ground and water are polluted?

    a. by bright lights

    b. by loud noises

    c. by plastic garbage

    d. by planes in the air

3. What is a way pollution hurts the planet?

    a. It makes the oceans dirty.

    b. It causes rain.

    c. It makes people live longer.

    d. Noises are too bright.

Name:_____ **Date:**_____

Directions: Read the chart, and answer the questions.

Ways to Help Earth

recycle

use a reusable water bottle

turn off lights when you leave the room

use a clothesline

conserve energy

don't waste food

minimize waste

plant a tree

use less water

unplug devices when you're done using them

ride a bike or walk

use cloth shopping bags

use energy-efficient light bulbs

compost

Geography

1. What is one way you can help Earth?

   a. use plastic shopping bags

   b. use more water for baths

   c. make sure you put cans in the garbage

   d. make sure the lights are out in the room

2. What are some ways you can make the planet cleaner?

   _____

   _____

   _____

3. What are some ways you can conserve water?

   _____

   _____

   _____

Geography

Name:_____ Date:_____

Directions: Read the text, and the study the graphic. Answer the questions.

Some clothing uses natural fibers, such as cotton. To grow cotton, you need land and water. The farmers use machines to harvest the cotton. These use fossil fuels. Human use of nature and what it takes to restore it is called an *ecological footprint*.

Our Ecological Footprint

Human-made structures:	**Agriculture:**	**Fishing:**	**Forests:**	**Grazing land:**	**Fossil fuels:**
houses	food	fish	logging	meat	manufacturing
roads	animal feed	shellfish	construction	dairy	transportation
bridges	biofuel	seaweed	furniture	products	heating
dams	textiles		paper	leather	cooling
factories			firewood	wool	

1. Which of the following affects a person's ecological footprint?

    a. the trees growing in the forest

    b. walking to the store

    c. the fish swimming in the ocean

    d. the cotton needed to make your clothes

2. What resources would be used to make paper?

    _____

    _____

    _____

3. What are some ways you could reduce your ecological footprint?

    _____

    _____

    _____

148

Name: _____ **Date:** _____

Directions: Draw a poster telling your fellow students about the impact your school is having on the environment and what they can do to help. Include at least three impacts and ways to reduce them.

Ways to Help the Environment

Recycle
aluminum cans.

Turn off lights
when you leave
a room.

Check for leaky
faucets.

Use reusable
bags for
shopping.

Geography

Name: _____ Date: _____

Economics

Directions: Read the text, and answer the questions.

> Scarcity is the difference between limited (scarce) resources and our wants and needs. All resources are limited, but our desire for resources is not. Different types of resources include natural ones, such as water, air, and oil. Other resources include things such as time and money.
>
> Scarcity is not the same everywhere and for everybody. People's incomes vary. They also have differing amounts of free time.

U.S. Seasonal Drought Outlook (2018)

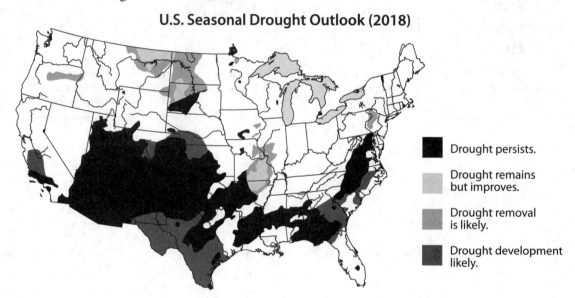

- ■ Drought persists.
- ▨ Drought remains but improves.
- ▨ Drought removal is likely.
- ■ Drought development likely.

1. Which of the following are examples of potential scarcity?

   a. fresh water after a hurricane   c. oil after an oil spill

   b. fresh air during a wild fire   d. all the above

2. What happens if you have a limited amount of time?

   a. You are able to spend all the time you want on an activity.

   b. You can spend all day playing computer games.

   c. You need to limit the time you text your friends.

   d. You can go to the mall all day.

3. Why is time a limited resource?

   a. We don't like to work too many hours before we have a break.

   b. We waste a lot of time doing other things we prefer.

   c. There are a limited number of hours in a day or week.

   d. It is hard to decide what to do with our time.

Name: _____ **Date:** _____

Directions: Read the text, and answer the questions.

Economics

Individuals, families, and countries make decisions about the resources they decide to use. They must consider the costs of their decisions. Costs are not just money. They include what is given up when making the decision. For example, time is a limited resource. You need to choose to do your homework or to spend time with your friends. Money is a limited resource. Your family might have to choose between a vacation and a new computer. Environmental controls can be expensive. A country may need to choose between a successful business that employs many people and clean water in the river beside the factory. A candy bar maker has a limited amount of chocolate. She must choose between making chocolate almond bars, chocolate caramel bars, or a mix. If she makes more of one bar, it means she must make fewer of the other.

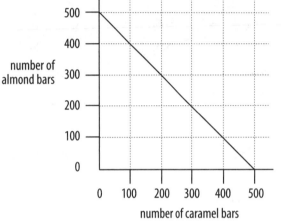

Number of Candy Bars

number of almond bars

number of caramel bars

1. Suppose a factory is being built on a river. The factory owners decide not to add environmental controls to protect the river. What are the possible results of this decision? Circle the two best answers.

   a. They might need new equipment to make their product.

   b. They might have to pay higher rent.

   c. They might kill animals and plants in the river.

   d. They might make a greater profit.

2. How might the candy maker decide which bars to make? Circle the two best answers.

   a. She could make the same amount of each kind.

   b. She could look at past sales.

   c. She could make a different candy.

   d. She could do something else.

3. A family has talked about whether to go on a trip or buy a new computer. How should they decide which one to pick?

   a. The children will decide.   c. They will ask someone else.

   b. The parents will decide.   d. They will flip a coin.

Economics

Name: _____ Date: _____

Directions: Study the images, and answer the questions.

residential yard next to a golf course in the desert   landscaping using conservation methods

1. Based on the images, what resource might be scarce in these communities?

   a. land

   b. clean air

   c. water

   d. food

2. What decision has each family made about their landscaping?

   _____

   _____

   _____

   _____

3. Which family is making a more environmentally responsible decision? Why?

   _____

   _____

   _____

   _____

   _____

Name:_____ Date:_____

Directions: Look at the image, and answer the questions.

1. What do you think they are deciding?

   a. which is heavier

   b. which to buy

   c. which looks better

   d. which is healthier

2. What factors could they be thinking about when they make their decision?

   _____

   _____

   _____

3. What factors are important when your family buys food?

   _____

   _____

   _____

   _____

Economics

Name:_____ **Date:**_____

Directions: You need to decide where your family will travel for a vacation. List the resources that you must consider before you make a decision. Which one of these three places will you choose? Why?

_____

_____

_____

_____

_____

_____

_____

_____

_____

51398—180 Days of Social Studies

© *Shell Education*

Name: _____ Date: _____

Directions: Read the text, and answer the questions.

Around the 12th century AD, a great civilization developed in the Andes. The Inkas conquered many different groups and made one people. They built superb roads. They developed agricultural methods. They spread their language and religion. Some people still speak their language today.

The emperor, who was called "the Inka," lived in Cuzco in Peru. People thought he was a god living on Earth. He and his nobles became very rich with gold and silver.

The Inkas were also great builders. Many of their creations are still scattered through South America. However, their civilization collapsed when the Spanish brought disease and war.

Inka ceremonial axe

1. Based on the text, what did the Inkas contribute to history?
   a. They had a god living on Earth.
   b. They defeated the Spanish.
   c. They developed agricultural methods.
   d. They used modern fishing techniques.

2. How do we know the Inkas were excellent engineers?
   a. They became very rich.
   b. They lived in the Andes.
   c. Parts of their buildings are still standing.
   d. They thought the emperor was a god.

3. Why does having a single language help a civilization?
   a. They can grow the same foods.
   b. They can believe in the same gods.
   c. They can build superb roads.
   d. They can communicate clearly.

History

Name: _____ Date: _____

Directions: Read the text, and answer the questions.

Several civilizations developed in the Americas. One of these was the Aztec. The Aztec people conquered the land of others. They were fierce fighters. They also learned from the cultures of people who had lived there before them. Their major city, Tenochtitlán, is now the site of Mexico City.

The people they conquered had to send treasures to Aztec leaders. They sent food, pottery, gold, and jewels. The Aztec also killed prisoners to please their gods. Many English words come from the Aztec. Words like *chili*, *avocado*, *chocolate*, *coyote*, and *guacamole* all come from the Aztec culture.

Mexican performing ancient Aztec dance

1. How did the Aztec take control of a large area of land?

   a. They bought land from others.

   b. They were fierce fighters.

   c. They built farms.

   d. They married local women.

2. Why did the conquered people have to give food, jewels, and gold?

   a. to show that they obeyed the Aztec

   b. to give away their excess

   c. to show they were rich

   d. to show they were good farmers

3. Why might English include some Aztec words?

   a. The Aztec rulers taught the words to the English explorers.

   b. Most English speakers really like chocolate and guacamole.

   c. English did not have words for those things, so they used local words.

   d. The words sounded very English.

Name: _____ **Date:** _____

Directions: Look at the web, and answer the questions.

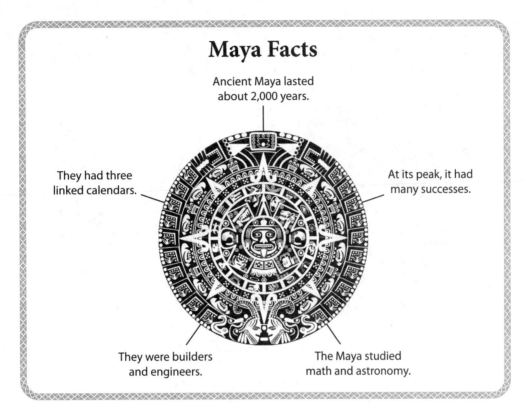

Maya Facts

Ancient Maya lasted about 2,000 years.

They had three linked calendars.

At its peak, it had many successes.

They were builders and engineers.

The Maya studied math and astronomy.

1. What can you deduce about the Maya people from the circle calendar?
   Circle all that apply.

   a. They liked art.

   b. They knew many details about the Earth.

   c. They knew the cycle repeated.

   d. They did not understand how a year works.

2. Why do you think the Maya needed to understand mathematics to make a calendar?

   _____

   _____

   _____

3. Do you think our calendar should be round like the Maya calendar? Explain why
   or why not.

   _____

   _____

History

Name: _____ Date: _____

Directions: Read the text, and answer the questions.

The Inkas built Machu Picchu before the Spanish explorers arrived. It is a vast complex of over 200 buildings high in the Andes Mountains.

Machu Picchu

1. The outside world did not learn about Machu Picchu until 1911. Based on the image, why do you think they did not find it?

   a. The local people kept it a secret.

   b. The Spanish didn't think it had gold or jewels.

   c. It was very high and hard to get to.

   d. No one was interested in seeing it.

2. Many tourists like to climb thousands of feet to reach Machu Picchu. Why do you think it is so fascinating?

   _____

   _____

3. Imagine you are a tourist in the year 2520. What natural or human-made landmark in the United States would you visit? Why?

   _____

   _____

   _____

Name:_____ Date:_____

Directions: Look at the image, and answer the question.

Moctezuma II was the last emperor of Mexico. He was defeated and killed by Hernán Cortés. The Spaniards then destroyed the Aztec civilization.

1. Tourists in Mexico sometimes get stomach bugs. They get germs from eating and drinking. This is called Moctezuma's Revenge. How do you think it got its name?

_____

_____

_____

_____

_____

_____

_____

History

Civics

Name:_____ Date:_____

Directions: Read the text, and answer the questions.

> There are many ways that we can do good things and show we care. Here are some ways to get involved in *civic participation*.
>
> - Work with your community to learn about people's needs and concerns.
> - Help to educate other people and get them involved. Help children who are new to your school.
> - Help people and communities directly, through cleaning up a park or volunteering to work in a community garden.
> - Make donations to charities or groups that help people.
> - Help to change laws that are hurtful to people, by actions such as writing petitions.
> - Form groups to influence companies. Work with them to improve social and environmental problems.

1. How might we learn about the needs and concerns of people in our community?
   a. Read a chapter book or novel.
   b. Watch the national news.
   c. Talk to people who live in the community.
   d. Play a video game.

2. How could we help people directly in a community?
   a. We could join sports teams.
   b. We could get a library card.
   c. We could do volunteer work.
   d. We could attend a concert.

3. Which of these could be directly helpful to people in need?
   a. writing an article for the newspaper
   b. writing in a personal journal
   c. building a new shopping mall
   d. making donations of food or clothing

Name: _____ **Date:** _____

Directions: Read the information. Then, answer the questions.

Bono is the lead singer of the famous Irish rock band U2. He has written many songs about troubles in the world and making it a better place. Bono and U2 have shown many ways to care for other people. In 1984, they raised money for starving people in Ethiopia. In 2006, they collected funds to help people affected by Hurricane Katrina.

Bono was one of the founders of a civic action group called ONE. Its members work toward ending severe poverty and disease in many countries. They petition governments to change laws and save people. The (RED) organization is part of ONE. It partners with large companies to fight AIDS, tuberculosis, and malaria. Bono has been given many awards to honor his civic engagement.

Civics

1. Who is Bono?
   a. He is a famous novelist from Britain.
   b. He is a famous politician from America.
   c. He is an Irish singer and social activist.
   d. He is a famous French playwright and writer.

2. What have Bono and U2 done have done to help people in need?
   a. helped people who were stranded on islands
   b. raised funds to build new amusement parks
   c. helped people who wanted to form large companies
   d. raised funds for people in need of food or medicine

3. What type of civic action has Bono chosen to be involved with?
   a. He works with his community to learn about people's interests.
   b. He helps to educate people about economic growth.
   c. He has helped clean up environmental oil spills.
   d. He works with groups to help people around the world.

Civics

Name: _____ Date: _____

Directions: Look at the web graphic. Then, answer the questions.

The Kielburgers

When he was 12 years old, Craig Kielburger, from Thornhill, Canada, read about a 12-year-old boy in Pakistan. He had been enslaved in a carpet factory. When he tried to tell about child slavery, he was murdered.

Today, Craig is an adult. He and his brother, Marc, run Free the Children, which is now called WE Charity. It has helped free thousands of children and open more than 100 schools. It trains teachers to help children with civic action.

Craig found out there were thousands of children enslaved. He wanted to make a difference. He started Free the Children to abolish child slave labor in the world.

Craig and his friends wrote petitions and faxed them to leaders of countries. They had bake sales and other events to raise money. They helped people around the world learn about enslaved children.

1. What first influenced Kielburger to become involved in helping others?

   a. He watched a movie about children who work.

   b. Someone told him about how people live in other countries.

   c. He read of a boy his age who was enslaved in another country.

   d. He visited a place where people were mistreated.

2. How did young Kielburger decide to make a difference?

   a. He got together with friends to clean up streets and parks.

   b. He wrote a book to tell about what he learned.

   c. He decided to go visit places he had read about.

   d. He started an organization to help stop enslavement.

3. How has Kielburger's social engagement made a difference in the world?

   _____

   _____

Name: _____ **Date:** _____

Directions: Read the text, and then answer the questions.

Malala Yousafzai was born in Pakistan, a country where girls have few rights. She loves learning, and her father made sure she could go to school.

But Taliban fighters took over her city. They made strict rules such as no television, no music, and no school for girls. Yousafzai bravely took action. She secretly started writing a blog for the BBC. She told about how terrible it was to live under Taliban rule.

Within a few years, the Pakistani army defeated away most of the Taliban. Yousafzai's school reopened, and she and other girls went back. This angered the Taliban, and a gunman shot Yousafzai. But she survived.

Since then, Yousafzai continues to take civic action to open schools and help girls get an education. She won the Nobel Peace Prize. She has spoken around the world with many leaders of countries. Her civic action has helped many.

1. Which of these is NOT true?

   a. Yousafzai was born in the Middle Eastern country of Pakistan.

   b. Pakistan is a country where girls have few rights.

   c. Yousafzai just gave up when the Taliban captured her city.

   d. The Taliban are radicals who restrict people's rights.

2. How has Yousafzai's civic engagement made a difference for people? If you were her, would you have made the same choices? Why?

   _____

   _____

3. If you could meet Yousafzai, what questions would you ask her? Why?

   _____

   _____

   _____

Civics

Name: _____ **Date:** _____

Directions: There are good and brave people in our world who take action to make a difference for others. Four of these are Bono, Craig and Marc Kielburger, and Malala Yousafzai. Tell about why they are people who set a good examples for us.

Bono

_____

_____

_____

_____

_____

_____

Craig and Marc Kielburger

_____

_____

_____

_____

_____

_____

Malala Yousafzai

_____

_____

_____

_____

_____

_____

51398—180 Days of Social Studies

Name: _____ **Date:** _____

Directions: Read the text, and answer the questions.

Human migration is the movement of people from one area to another for the purpose of settling somewhere new. There are many reasons why people migrate to a new region. These reasons can be grouped into four main categories: environmental, economic, cultural, and political. These factors are called push and pull forces. They either push people to leave an area, or they pull people to go to a new region.

Sometimes people migrate by choice, such as moving somewhere for a new job. Other times, the migration is by force, such as moving due to war. Migration usually happens for a combination of these push and pull factors.

1. Based on the text, which factors affect migration? Circle all that apply.

    a. culture

    b. politics

    c. economics

    d. transport

2. Why are the reasons for human migration called "push" and "pull" factors?

    a. They encourage people to migrate.

    b. They encourage families to stay.

    c. They are factors that make people want to stay.

    d. They are reasons that draw someone in or force them to move.

3. What do you think is an economic reason to migrate?

    a. There is family in another country.

    b. The migrator's family moved away.

    c. There are more jobs in another area.

    d. The migrator's religion is oppressed.

Name: _____ **Date:** _____

Geography

Directions: Read the text, and study the pie chart. Answer the questions.

People migrate around the United States and from other countries. The safety and job prospects in the United States encourage many people to immigrate here. There are policies in place to help control who can move here.

People come to the United States to live, study, or work. This has been a major part of the country's history, population growth, and diversity.

The United States has a large number of immigrants. In 2015, 47 million of the people who were living in the United States had been born in another country.

U.S. New, Legal, Permanent Residents, 2015

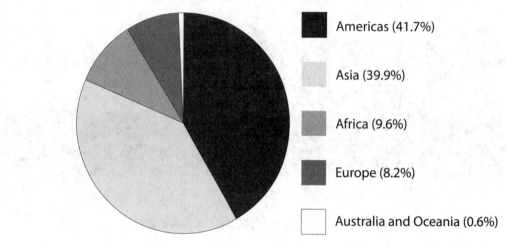

- Americas (41.7%)
- Asia (39.9%)
- Africa (9.6%)
- Europe (8.2%)
- Australia and Oceania (0.6%)

1. Where did the second-biggest group of legal, permanent residents come from in 2015?

   a. Africa

   b. Asia

   c. Americas

   d. Europe

2. Based on the text, why do people come to America?

   a. safety

   b. work

   c. school

   d. all the above

3. How has immigration helped population growth?

   a. People move around regions.

   b. People move and have families.

   c. People have been settling near work and places to study.

   d. People have been moving to America throughout its history.

Name: _____ Date: _____

Directions: Study the graphic, and answer the questions.

Push and Pull Factors in Human Migration

PUSH →

PULL →

- few services
- lack of jobs
- unhappy life
- poor transportation system
- natural disaster
- war
- food shortage

- access to services
- jobs
- more leisure choices
- better transport links
- better living conditions
- hope for the future
- family links

1. What is a reason someone would leave their country? Circle all that apply.

   a. access to services

   b. an abundance of food

   c. stable government

   d. better living conditions somewhere else

2. Why would living conditions be both a "push" and "pull" factor?

   _____

   _____

   _____

3. Explain why one category is called "push" and the other "pull."

   _____

   _____

   _____

51398—180 Days of Social Studies

Name:_____ Date:_____

Directions: Read the text, and study the graphic. Answer the questions.

Geography

Ancestry is your family history. It is where you come from. It usually looks at the origins of your family from a long time ago, not just your parents or grandparents. Many people study where they came from as a hobby.

15 Largest Ancestries in the United States, 2000

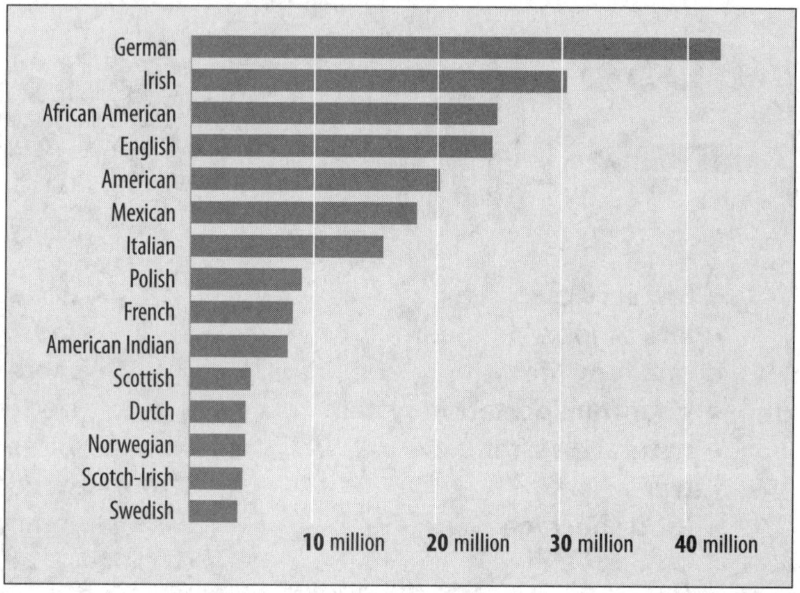

German	
Irish	
African American	
English	
American	
Mexican	
Italian	
Polish	
French	
American Indian	
Scottish	
Dutch	
Norwegian	
Scotch-Irish	
Swedish	

10 million   20 million   30 million   40 million

1. In the graph above, which country is most highly represented?

   a. Ireland   **c.** France

   b. Mexico   **d.** Germany

2. Think about your family history. Has your family lived in different states or countries? If so, which ones? If not, why do you think they didn't migrate?

   _____

   _____

   _____

3. If you were to leave your state or the country, where would you go? Why?

   _____

   _____

   _____

Name: _____ **Date:** _____

Directions: Look at the graphic, and answer the question.

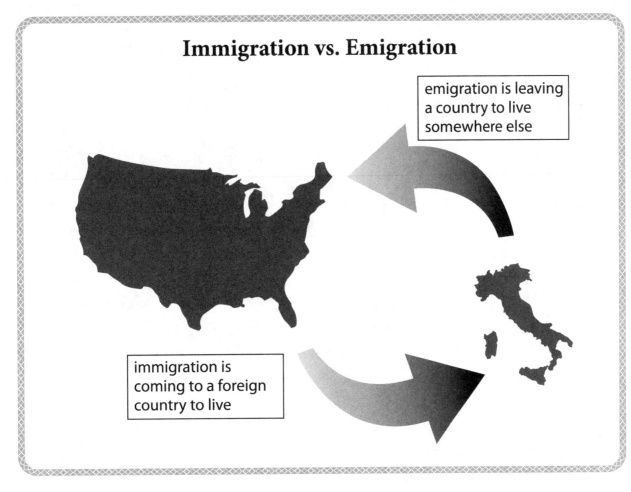

Immigration vs. Emigration

emigration is leaving a country to live somewhere else

immigration is coming to a foreign country to live

1. Explain two reasons people immigrate to the United States and two reasons people may emigrate from the United States.

_____

_____

_____

_____

_____

_____

Name: _____ Date: _____

Economics

Directions: Read the text, and answer the questions.

There are several types of economic activity. These are called sectors. The first sector uses resources from the earth. Farming, fishing, and mining are part of this sector. The second sector is goods that are made. Manufacturing and construction are in this sector. A third sector is services. Some of these services, such as stores, help people get their goods. Other services include things like banks and tourism. The government also provides services.

Early civilizations were mostly based on the first sector. In the past, most people in the United States had jobs that came from the first sector. This has changed. Today many people have service jobs.

1. Which sector includes people who access the earth's natural resources directly?

   a. second sector

   b. third sector

   c. first sector

   d. none of the above

2. Why did early civilizations mostly have economies based on the first sector?

   a. They were learning to make new products.

   b. They were mostly hunter-gatherers or agricultural.

   c. They did not want to develop a lot of expensive technology.

   d. People did not need a service industry.

3. Which of the following are in the third sector?

   a. farmer

   b. taxi driver

   c. factory worker

   d. miner

Name: _____ **Date:** _____

Directions: Read the text, and answer the questions.

Economics

The rich natural resources of North America brought Europeans here. The first settlers, like the natives, were mostly producers in the first sector. They grew food. They found resources for trade, such as furs. In 1800, 80 to 90 percent of people worked in farming and other first-sector jobs. Many people moved west and settled new areas so they could get land to farm. By 1900, just under half of all Americans lived on farms. Then, huge changes in technology reduced the need for first-sector workers.

By 2000, less than 2 percent of workers had farm jobs. Modern farms are much more efficient. They produce larger quantities of food. Today, there are some small family farms. But many farms are big businesses.

1. Which of the following are first-sector jobs?

   a. farming

   b. chef

   c. programmer

   d. construction

2. Why did many people move farther west in the 1800s?

   a. to get away from growing cities

   b. to get married

   c. to get land to farm

   d. to get a job

3. Why are there fewer agricultural jobs today?

   a. People don't own the land.

   b. People don't know how to run a farm.

   c. Technology does many of the old jobs.

   d. There isn't enough land.

Economics

Name: _____ **Date:** _____

Directions: Study the pie chart, and answer the questions.

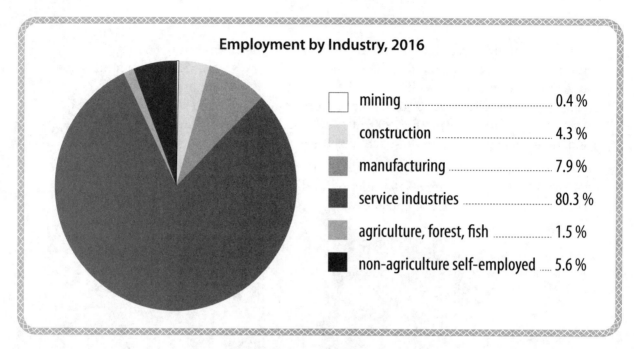

Employment by Industry, 2016

☐	mining	0.4 %
	construction	4.3 %
	manufacturing	7.9 %
	service industries	80.3 %
	agriculture, forest, fish	1.5 %
	non-agriculture self-employed	5.6 %

1. Which of the industries in this pie chart make goods?

   a. construction

   b. agriculture

   c. mining

   d. forestry

2. Where do people get manufactured goods?

   a. online or in a store

   b. from home

   c. from a mine

   d. in the forest

3. Manufacturing provided 9.5 percent of the jobs in 2006. What do you think happened over the next 10 years?

   _____

   _____

   _____

   _____

Name: _____ **Date:** _____

Directions: Look at the graphic, and answer the questions.

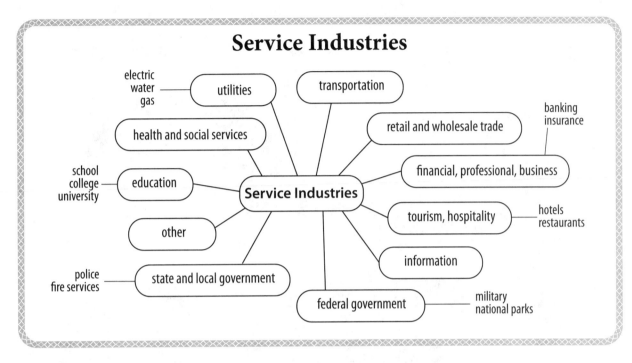

Service Industries

1. Which of the following is NOT a service job?

    a. taxi driver

    b. doctor

    c. baker

    d. massage therapist

2. Why are these called service industries?

    _____

    _____

    _____

3. Which of these service industries has been part of your life today?

    _____

    _____

    _____

    _____

Name: _____ **Date:**_____

Directions: Look at the image, and answer the question.

Economics

1. Explain the services you see in the picture.

_____

_____

_____

_____

_____

_____

_____

_____

_____

51398—180 Days of Social Studies

© *Shell Education*

Name: _____ Date: _____

Directions: Read the text, and answer the questions.

History

The Silk Road was a series of trade routes between Europe and Asia. Some were across land and others by sea. Merchants used it between 200 BC and AD 1500. Preferred goods for trade were light and easy to carry. These included spices, silk, gems, and precious metals. The Silk Road was a difficult and dangerous route. The Ottoman Empire collected money by forcing traders to pay taxes when they passed through. That increased the cost of the goods for buyers and sellers both. As a result, several European countries began to dream of other routes to the riches in the East.

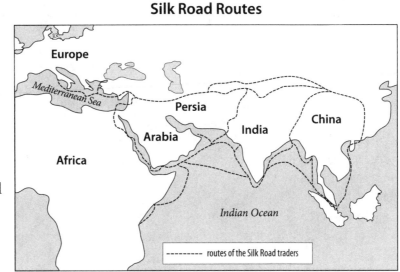

Silk Road Routes

Europe

Mediterranean Sea

Persia

China

Arabia

India

Africa

Indian Ocean

-------- routes of the Silk Road traders

1. Why were Asian trade goods expensive in Europe?

   a. They were easy to carry.

   b. The traders had to pay taxes.

   c. Goods did not make the trip to Europe.

   d. The trade routes were easy.

2. Why did Europeans want to find different routes?

   a. They wanted to charge more.

   b. They were bored by the Silk Road.

   c. They wanted a less expensive and dangerous route.

   d. The Silk Road was too well known.

3. Why did the Ottoman Empire charge taxes?

   a. It did not like people passing through.

   b. It could make money from foreigners.

   c. It wanted the goods the merchants carried.

   d. It didn't want the merchants to make money.

51398—180 Days of Social Studies

Name:_____ **Date:**_____

Directions: Study the timeline, and answer the questions.

Age of European Discovery Timeline

| 1482 | 1492 | 1499–1502 | 1576–1578 |

Diogo Cão was the first European to sail into the Congo River and farther south along the African coast. This led to later Portuguese colonies and establishing the African slave trade.

Christopher Columbus reached the Caribbean Islands (North America).

Amerigo Vespucci sailed down the coast of South America to Argentina. He realized this was a "New World." America was named for him.

Martin Frobisher led three unsuccessful expeditions to find a Northwest Passage to the Indies. He sailed only as far as Baffin Island, where Frobisher Bay was named for him.

1. Based on the timeline, which explorer was partially responsible for the beginnings of the African slave trade?

   a. Amerigo Vespucci

   b. Martin Frobisher

   c. Diogo Cão

   d. Christopher Columbus

2. How did the Americas get their name?

   a. It was a name given by the native peoples.

   b. People voted on their favorite name.

   c. They were named after Amerigo Vespucci.

   d. Christopher Columbus named them.

3. Why is Martin Frobisher remembered in history?

   a. He found the Northwest Passage to Asia.

   b. He succeeded in reaching the Indies.

   c. He sailed all the way to Baffin Island.

   d. He led three successful expeditions to the Northwest Passage.

51398—180 Days of Social Studies

© *Shell Education*

Name: _____ Date: _____

Directions: Look at the map, and answer the questions.

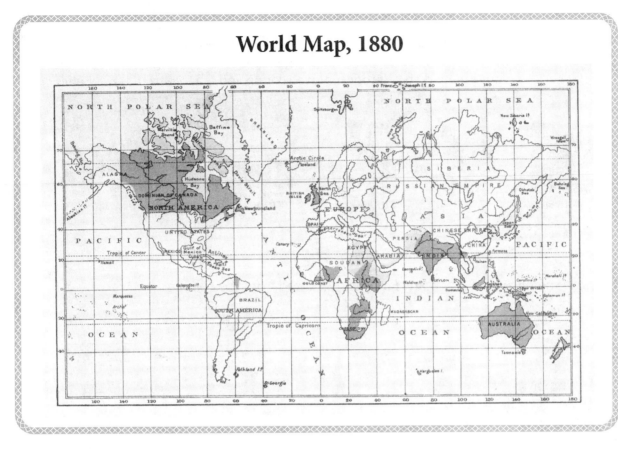

World Map, 1880

1. Based on the map, which continents had British settlements?

   a. Asia

   b. Africa

   c. Australia

   d. all the above

2. If a British officer visited each of the colonies, what type of temperatures do you think would he experience in most colonies? Why?

   _____

   _____

   _____

3. Why would it be difficult for Great Britain to rule all these places?

   _____

   _____

   _____

History

Name:_____ Date:_____

Directions: Look at the images and text, and answer the questions.

> Trade develops when people want or need goods they do not have where they live. Many people moved to the American colonies to grow or obtain trade goods they could send back to European markets. Europeans loved cotton and tabacco from the colonies.

| beaver felt hat | fish | timber | cotton | corn | tobacco |

1. Circle the two items that many Europeans wanted from the colonies.

   a. fish

   b. cotton

   c. tobacco

   d. timber

2. Beaver pelts were used to make hats. Why were these wants rather than needs for the Europeans?

   _____

   _____

   _____

   _____

3. What are some of your wants that come through trade with other countries?

   _____

   _____

   _____

   _____

51398—180 Days of Social Studies

Name: _____ **Date:** _____

Directions: Look at the images, and answer the question.

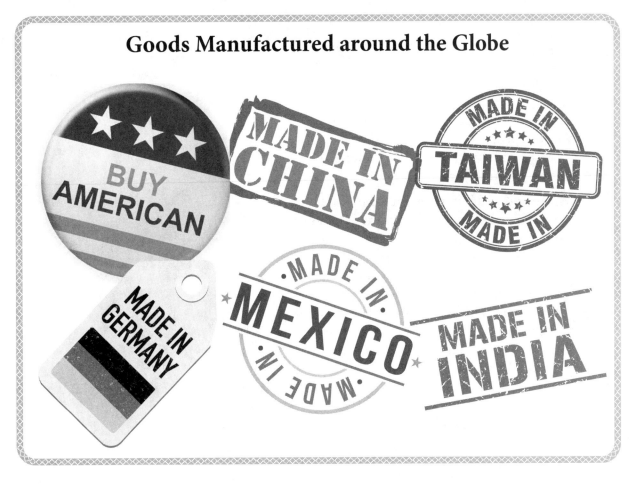

Goods Manufactured around the Globe

1. Why do you think people choose to buy goods made in other countries instead of goods made in the United States?

_____

_____

_____

_____

_____

_____

_____

Civics

Name: _____ Date: _____

Directions: Read the text, and answer the questions.

Ryan White was a teenager from Indiana. He often needed blood transfusions because of an illness called hemophilia. In 1984, he got HIV/AIDS from infected blood. After a while, with medication, he was well enough to return to school. But people thought they might "catch" the disease and refused to let White attend. He and his parents took legal action and won.

White returned but was shunned by other students and people in his community. His story gained national attention. He bravely became a spokesperson and advocated for improved blood testing and care. Sadly, White died at the age of 18. That year, the president of the United States signed *The Ryan White CARE Act* to fund testing, care, and treatment for Americans with AIDS.

AIDS awareness ribbon

1. How did White get HIV/AIDS?
   a. He got it by shaking someone's hand.
   b. He got it by sharing food.
   c. He was in the same room as a sick person.
   d. He got it through a blood transfusion.

2. What happened when White was well enough to return to school?
   a. He was invited back to class.
   b. He joined the football team.
   c. He was not allowed to attend.
   d. He made many friends when he returned.

3. How did White's civic work help other people?
   a. People learned more about cancer and hemophilia.
   b. A law was passed to help people with AIDS.
   c. People were scared of others with AIDS.
   d. People learned to shun those with AIDS.

Name: _____ **Date:** _____

Directions: Read the text. Then, circle all answers that are correct.

Civics

Dr. Temple Grandin was diagnosed with autism when she was two years old. Her mother worked hard to find her teachers who could help her learn to speak and learn. Grandin talked by the time she was four, but she continued to struggle socially throughout school. She was often teased because she was different.

Still, Grandin worked hard and earned degrees in psychology and animal sciences. She became a consultant for companies with slaughterhouses. She guided them to improve the quality of life for animals. She then became a university professor.

Grandin has become well-known for speaking up for people with autism and their education. She also promotes animal rights. She has written many books to tell about how people with autism feel and think. Grandin has been given degrees and awards for her civic works.

Temple Grandin

1. Who is Temple Grandin?
   a. a person who improves the lives of people and animals
   b. a person who makes friends easily
   c. a person who has earned degrees in human medicine
   d. a person who never got teased

2. Which of these are some of Grandin's accomplishments?
   a. She invented new technology.
   b. She went to community college.
   c. She taught companies to improve the quality of life for animals.
   d. She is a farmer.

3. What type of civic action has Grandin chosen to be involved with?
   a. working with groups to donate toward people in need
   b. helping to educate people about democracy
   c. helping to educate people about autism and animal rights
   d. working with her community to educate about recycling

Name: _____ Date: _____

Directions: Look at the graphic. Then, answer the questions.

Civics

Jimmy Carter, thirty-ninth president of the United States, and Rosalynn Carter founded the Carter Center in 1982.

The Carter Center's Goals

Resolve conflicts in many countries

Support rule of law and justice in other countries

Offer health programs to
- fight diseases
- support mother and baby health
- help with mental health issues
- prevent blindness (from parasites)

Defend human rights and equality

Oversee elections in countries with developing democracies

Give people access to information

1. Which of these is true?

   a. The Carters founded a recreation center.

   b. Jimmy Carter was the vice president of the United States.

   c. The Carters wanted to help other people around the world.

   d. The Carter Center work is done only in the United States.

2. How did the Carters choose to take civic action?

   _____

   _____

3. Why do you think it would be important to oversee elections in some countries?

   _____

   _____

   _____

Name: _____ **Date:** _____

Directions: Read the text, and then answer the questions.

Rosa Parks began standing up for people's rights in Alabama during the 1950s. At that time, African Americans did not have equal access to many services in some states. For instance, they had to go to separate schools and sit at the backs of buses.

One day, Parks refused to give up her bus seat to a white person. She was tired of being discriminated against. The driver had Parks arrested. That evening, the local NAACP arranged a boycott. They invited Dr. Martin Luther King Jr. to lead. African Americans were asked to protest and stop taking buses.

The boycott lasted 381 days. It was a dangerous time. Some white people took revenge by burning churches and homes. Finally, the U.S. Supreme Court made the city give equal rights to all people. Parks made a difference for many people.

Rosa Parks

Civics

1. Which of these is NOT true?

   a. Parks was an African American from Alabama.

   b. Parks had been discriminated against all her life.

   c. Parks believed discrimination was acceptable.

   d. Parks had been sitting at the backs of buses all her life.

2. Why was Parks arrested? Do you believe this was fair treatment? Why?

   _____

   _____

   _____

3. In what ways is Parks an inspiration for others?

   _____

   _____

Name: _____ **Date:** _____

Directions: Which of these Americans do you admire most? Why? What actions could you take to be more like them?

Civics

Ryan White

_____

_____

_____

_____

_____

Temple Grandin

_____

_____

_____

_____

_____

Rosa Parks

_____

_____

_____

_____

_____

Name: _____ **Date:** _____

Directions: Read the text, and answer the questions.

Geographers look at past and present patterns to plan for the future. For example, they look at where people live and what they use to plan how communities will grow.

They look at physical patterns in the earth's crust and how it moves. They look at resources such as forests and ecosystems. Geographers also consider cultural patterns, such as an area's history and where its boundaries are. They must also consider and work to preserve land that is protected. Protected areas are places that have something special needs to be preserved. National parks, such as Yellowstone, are protected areas.

Yellowstone National Park

1. How do geographers plan for community growth?
   a. They want to build in national parks.
   b. They don't look at patterns for planning.
   c. They look at how and what people use.
   d. They look at building designs.

2. How do geographers use patterns?
   a. They can see how people use the area.
   b. They use patterns to find rivers and lakes.
   c. They look at the trees and plants.
   d. They look at how buildings change.

3. Why are boundaries important when planning cities?
   a. to show where parks and forests are
   b. to show where the community can grow
   c. to help planners find public transportation
   d. to help planners find out how the earth moves

Geography

Name: _____   Date: _____

Directions: Read the text, and answer the questions.

In the past, society was based mainly on farming. Farming areas are called rural areas. But now, the world's population is over 50 percent urban. An urban area is a city or town. This shift means that geographers need to look at land use as it changes to mainly urban spaces.

Urban planners look at changes in land use. They plan for how communities will grow and be managed. They study whether planned buildings will work with the area. They consider environmental concerns, traffic, zoning, and other factors. They also look at economic, environmental, and social trends.

Change in Rural and Urban Population Size, 1910–2010

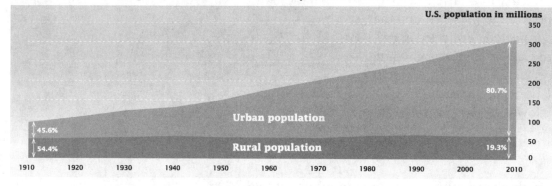

1. How has population changed over time?
   a. Communities are now focused on farming.
   b. Communities are now more urban than rural.
   c. Communities are now mostly commercial.
   d. Communities now have fewer people.

2. Based on the text, what are some ways urban planners look at growth? Circle all that apply.
   a. They look at traffic flow.
   b. They look at zoning.
   c. They look at weather.
   d. They look at growth.

3. Why are economic concerns important?
   a. to make sure farms are thriving
   b. to keep communities financially strong
   c. to ensure people can drive well
   d. to keep the proper zoning

Name:_____ Date:_____

Directions: Study the graphic, and answer the questions.

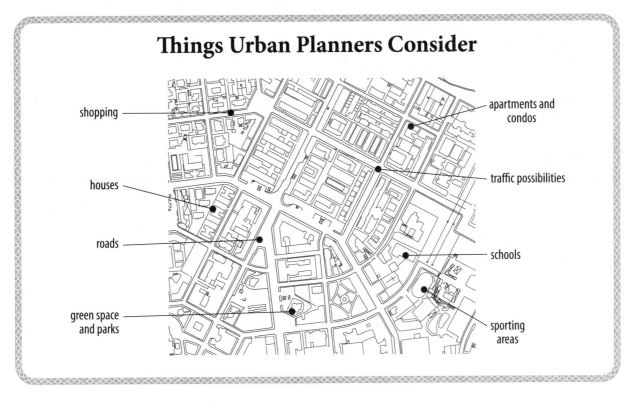

Things Urban Planners Consider

shopping

apartments and condos

houses

traffic possibilities

roads

schools

green space and parks

sporting areas

1. Which of these is NOT a concern of urban planners?

   a. access to green space

   b. traffic patterns

   c. weather

   d. recreation areas

2. Where apartments and houses are located affects traffic. Why do you think this is?

   _____

   _____

   _____

3. What three things do you think are most important for urban planners to consider?

   _____

   _____

   _____

Name:_____ **Date:**_____

Geography

Directions: Read the text, and answer the questions.

A lot of thought went into your community and how people get around in it. The roads were carefully planned for traffic flow and ease of getting from place to place. Transportation planners look at where to put highways, where to install stop lights, and where bridges should be. Pedestrians need to be considered as well. Planners look at which roads get sidewalks and where pedestrian crossings should be.

Public transportation also needs to be considered. Some large cities have subways or trains. Most cities have buses, all designed to move large groups of people around.

1. Why is transportation planning important?

   a. to have access to shopping

   b. to help people get around quickly and safely

   c. to keep the community economically sound

   d. to know where people are going

2. What forms of public transportation does your community have? Do you think you need more public transportation? Why or why not?

   _____

   _____

   _____

3. Think about your community. Is it well set up for walking? If so, in what ways? If not, what could be done to improve it?

   _____

   _____

   _____

51398—180 Days of Social Studies © *Shell Education*

Name: _____ **Date:** _____

Directions: Examine the photos, and answer the question.

City Growth

transportation

_____

housing

_____

green space

_____

office space

_____

1. What do urban planners consider when planning for city growth? Pick three of these ways, and explain why they are important.

_____

_____

_____

_____

_____

_____

Name: _____ **Date:** _____

Directions: Read the text, and answer the questions.

Economics

Producers and consumers in different countries buy from and sell to each other. This is international trade. It can give consumers access to new products. Some may be goods that are not produced in their own countries. Trade encourages competition. This may lower prices.

When producers sell their products to another country, they are exporting the goods. When a country brings in goods produced by another country, it is importing the goods. The United States is a major exporter and importer of goods. The federal government is in charge of international trade. This was decided by the Founding Fathers. They put trade in the Constitution.

1. Why are some international products different from things produced in the United States?
   a. The exporters want to accept lower prices.
   b. The exporters get rid of things they can't sell at home.
   c. Some products may not be produced in the United States
   d. Some products may be too expensive to import.

2. Why might trade lead to lower prices?
   a. People will buy what is in the store.
   b. The imported products may be cheaper than American products.
   c. Trade will never lower prices.
   d. Adding taxed may increase the prices.

3. Why is the federal government in charge of international trade in the United States?
   a. They have all the trade experts.
   b. The United States is a command economy.
   c. The Constitution says this is a federal responsibility.
   d. The Constitution says that the states should control trade.

Name:_____ **Date:**_____

Directions: Read the text, and answer the questions.

Free trade is the idea that countries should be able to import and export goods with no rules. Supply and demand can decide prices. Some people think that trade needs to be managed. They feel that supply and demand may not lead to the best results for the people in a country.

Corn crops receive federal subsidies.

Governments make rules to control trade. Sometimes they put taxes on imported goods. This makes them more expensive, so manufacturers within the country can compete. They also give subsidies. A subsidy is money given by the government to help local producers. Subsidies are common in agriculture in the United States.

1. What does free trade mean?
   a. supply and demand managed by government
   b. agricultural goods
   c. money for goods
   d. no rules on trade

2. What may happen if the United States placed more taxes on imported shoes?
   a. Imported shoes may cost more.
   b. Imported shoes may cost less.
   c. People may buy more imported shoes.
   d. Extra taxes will not change anything.

3. What may be a benefit of free trade?
   a. There will be fewer goods available.
   b. There will be more tax dollars for the government.
   c. People will have less choice in the stores.
   d. Consumers and producers decide prices.

Economics

Name: _____ **Date:** _____

Directions: Study the graph, and answer the questions.

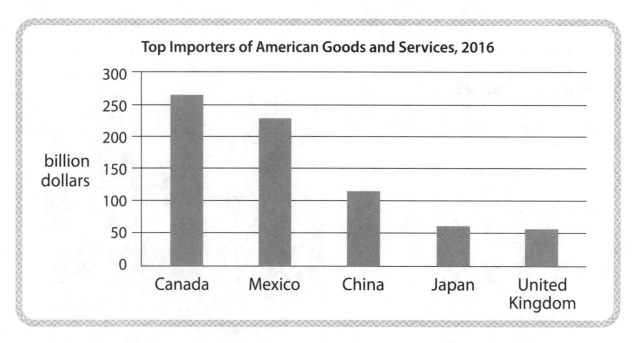

Top Importers of American Goods and Services, 2016

billion dollars (y-axis: 0, 50, 100, 150, 200, 250, 300)

Categories: Canada, Mexico, China, Japan, United Kingdom

1. Why is Canada important for many American businesses that produce exports?

   a. Canada is a neighboring country.

   b. Most Canadians speak English.

   c. Canada is the biggest purchaser of U.S. exports.

   d. Canada had a dollar-based currency.

2. Why are Canada and Mexico good customers for American companies?

   _____

   _____

   _____

3. In 2016, China imported about $116 billion worth of U.S. exports. The United States imported about $463 billion worth of Chinese exports. Why might this unbalance of trade hurt the United States?

   _____

   _____

   _____

Name:_____ Date:_____

Directions: Look at the graphs, and answer the questions.

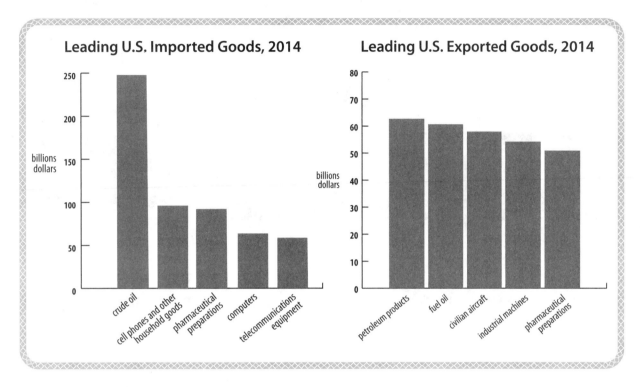

Leading U.S. Imported Goods, 2014

Leading U.S. Exported Goods, 2014

Economics

1. Which of these statements about the United States is correct?

   a. The United States exports more machines than fuel oil.

   b. The major exports and imports are the same in value.

   c. The United States exports more pharmaceuticals than petroleum products.

   d. The United States imports more crude oil than computers.

2. Why do you think the United States imports a lot of crude oil?

   _____

   _____

   _____

3. Which categories of imports are most important to you?

   _____

   _____

   _____

Economics

Name: _____ **Date:** _____

Directions: Look at the graphic, and answer the question.

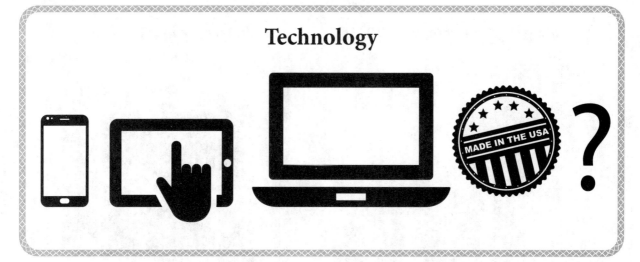

Technology

1. Why are so many computers, smartphones, and accessories imported rather than made in the United States? How could that be changed?

_____

_____

_____

_____

_____

_____

_____

_____

_____

_____

_____

51398—180 Days of Social Studies

© *Shell Education*

ANSWER KEY *(cont.)*

Week 1—History

Day 1
1. b
2. d
3. d

Day 2
1. c
2. a
3. d (allow for b)

Day 3
1. b
2. c
3. Responses will vary but may include food was plentiful; there was a wide variety of foods available.

Day 4
1. a
2. Responses will vary but may include they did not move often; and they had time to make and collect more things.
3. Responses will vary but may include that we don't need as many things as we have.

Day 5
1. Responses will vary.
2. Responses will vary but may include that today people have many conveniences that make their lives better and easier.

Week 2—Civics

Day 1
1. d
2. b
3. c

Day 2
1. b
2. c
3. d

Day 3
1. d
2. c
3. Responses will vary but may include that we have a democratic republic; people who are 18 years or older and who are American citizens can vote.

Day 4
1. c
2. Responses will vary but may include that they fought for independence; they created a new government to allow more freedom for citizens.
3. Responses will vary but may include that the beliefs of the people of Ancient Athens, John Locke, and the colonists influenced the Constitution; the ideas were democracy, rights to life, liberty, and property, and independence.

Day 5
Responses will vary but may include the following:
1. Early democracy in ancient Athens: Citizens voted on everything; they did not elect representatives to vote for them on laws; only men who had military training were considered to be citizens; and only citizens could vote.
2. Before democracy in the American colonies: The colonists were overtaxed; their rights were not protected; they wanted a new government.
3. Early ideas that had an impact on the Constitution: democracy; rights to life, liberty, and property; and independence.

Week 3—Geography

Day 1
1. d
2. b
3. c

Day 2
1. a
2. a, c
3. c

ANSWER KEY *(cont.)*

Day 3
1. a
2. d
3. Responses will vary.

Day 4
1. c
2. Responses will vary but should include a location that is accessible but not too obvious and that can be protected from bad weather.
3. Responses will vary.

Day 5
1. Responses will vary.

Week 4—Economics

Day 1
1. a
2. b
3. d

Day 2
1. b
2. c
3. a

Day 3
1. b
2. b
3. Responses will vary but may include eat them quickly; not grow as much of that food, etc.

Day 4
1. a, b
2. Responses will vary but may include pickling (e.g., pickles); salting (e.g., ham or bacon); and drying (e.g., fruits).
3. Responses will vary but may include freezing and canning.

Day 5
1. Responses will vary but may include reduced need for hunting; allowed for surplus; and used for travel, tilling land, and carrying loads.

Week 5—History

Day 1
1. d
2. b
3. a

Day 2
1. d
2. a
3. Responses will vary but may include fertile land is important for growing food.

Day 3
1. d
2. c

Day 4
1. b
2. Responses will vary but may include harshness of Hammurabi compared to today; use of capital and corporal punishment and imprisonment; and reference to slavery.
3. Responses will vary but may include that they were cruel long ago; and reference to slavery.

Day 5
1. Responses will vary but may include collecting information; sharing laws; and keeping track of trade.

Week 6—Civics

Day 1
1. c
2. d
3. b

Day 2
1. a, d
2. b
3. b

ANSWER KEY *(cont.)*

Day 3

1. b
2. Citizens had rights to vote, marry, run a business, and be elected to office.
3. Responses will vary but may include that the Consul was very powerful but had huge responsibility; while citizens had less power or responsibility, they did have rights.

Day 4

1. b
2. Responses will vary but may relate to defending people's rights and promoting the common good; helping those who cannot help themselves.
3. Responses will vary but may include that people generally prefer to make up their own minds.

Day 5

1. Responses will vary but may include that ancient Rome was smaller and simpler; but both governments offered rules and responsibilities for citizens.

Week 7—Geography

Day 1

1. a
2. d
3. c

Day 2

1. d
2. a
3. b

Day 3

1. d
2. c
3. Responses will vary.

Day 4

1. c
2. Responses will vary but may include that mapmakers can use computers, satellites, etc.
3. Responses will vary but may include that urban areas are denser, so more complicated.

Day 5

1. Responses will vary but may include shopping downtown (city map); traveling around the world (atlas); camping (compass); and driving to a different city (GPS).

Week 8—Economics

Day 1

1. b
2. a, b, c
3. d

Day 2

1. c
2. a
3. Responses will vary but may include tools; surplus food; large population.

Day 3

1. d
2. Responses will vary but may include that they would be exposed to new ideas and foods.
3. Responses will vary but may include that you wouldn't know its purpose; wouldn't want to use it.

Day 4

1. b
2. Responses will vary but may include it was lighter; it was easier to make.
3. Responses will vary but may include things that are important to the student.

Day 5

1. Response should include land and sea routes, mixed routes; examples will vary.

Week 9—History

Day 1
1. a
2. c
3. b

Day 2
1. b
2. c
3. d

Day 3
1. b
2. c
3. Responses will vary but may include that the Israelites believed that the commandments come from god.

Day 4
1. c
2. Approximately 3,300 years; 1,300 years plus the current date.
3. Responses will vary but may include the ability of people to get along and respect each other.

Day 5
1. Responses will vary but may include that they wanted to end the Israelites' religion and convert them; it was not effective; Judaism is still a religion today; many people still visit and pray at the wall.

Week 10—Civics

Day 1
1. b
2. d
3. d

Day 2
1. c
2. c
3. a

Day 3
1. d
2. Responses will vary but may include that it was ruled by Hitler and the Nazis; the leader's power was unlimited; and he hurt and killed many people.
3. Responses will vary but may include that the country is governed by one party; the people do not have freedoms.

Day 4
1. d
2. Responses may vary but should include the 15th Amendment, which states that all people have rights, regardless of race, color, or previous standing.
3. Responses will vary.

Day 5
1. Responses will vary but should include that the United States is a democracy where citizens have rights and responsibilities; China is a dictatorship where citizens have very few rights.

Week 11—Geography

Day 1
1. b
2. d

Day 2
1. a
2. b
3. a

Day 3
1. b
2. c
3. Responses will vary.

Day 4
1. c
2. Arizona or Texas—hottest summer; Minnesota—coolest winter (also could be North Dakota or Maine)
3. Responses will vary.

Day 5
1. Responses will vary.

Week 12—Economics

Day 1
1. a
2. c
3. c

Day 2
1. d
2. b
3. a

Day 3
1. c
2. Responses will vary but may include to increase profits and reduce costs.
3. Responses will vary but may include that people don't work hard or quit and go where working conditions are better.

Day 4
1. b
2. Responses will vary but may include counterfeiting; value of the money.
3. Responses will vary.

Day 5
1. Responses will vary.

Week 13—History

Day 1
1. c
2. d
3. b

Day 2
1. a
2. a
3. a

Day 3
1. c
2. c
3. Responses will vary but may include that women were considered less important than men.

Day 4
1. c
2. Responses will vary but may include that they were well provided; and had time for leisure.
3. Responses will vary but may include philosophy, mathematics, democracy, and Olympics.

Day 5
1. Responses will vary.

Week 14—Civics

Day 1
1. b
2. b
3. d

Day 2
1. b
2. c
3. c

Day 3
1. c
2. Responses will vary but should include that the government would deal with the president, who is in charge of policy for his country and dealing with other countries.
3. Responses will vary but should include that the president was responsible because he was in charge of the military.

Day 4
1. c
2. Responses will vary but should include that our legislative branch can make laws and impeach government officials; it is part of the "checks and balances" system; the Russian legislative branch does not have these powers.
3. Responses will vary but should include an American court; you would have the right to a fair trial; people's rights are not always respected in Russia.

ANSWER KEY (cont.)

Day 5

1. Responses will vary but should include that the American Constitution guarantees the rights and freedoms of citizens; rights are not always respected in Russia; Congress may vote to limit trade relations if human rights are not respected.

Week 15—Geography

Day 1
1. b
2. a
3. c

Day 2
1. b
2. a
3. d

Day 3
1. d
2. Responses will vary but may include that there is enough rainfall and fertile soil to support forest growth.
3. Responses will vary but may include that adequate rainfall is needed for forest and grasslands to grow; without it, there is desert.

Day 4
1. d
2. Responses will vary but should include that climate is measured over a longer period of time; weather is current.
3. Responses will vary.

Day 5
1. Responses will vary but may include that features such as mountains and swamps are bad for settlement; railroads and rivers can provide transportation; forests can provide wood.

Week 16—Economics

Day 1
1. b
2. d
3. c

Day 2
1. b
2. b
3. a, b

Day 3
1. d
2. c
3. Responses will vary but may include that they don't work very well; people don't like them.

Day 4
1. c
2. Responses will vary but should include that there are fewer command economies in the world.
3. Responses will vary but should include that the United States is among the free market economies.

Day 5
1. Responses will vary but should include a free market system.

Week 17—History

Day 1
1. a
2. c
3. a

Day 2
1. d
2. c
3. b

Day 3
1. c
2. d
3. Responses will vary but may include that they were imaginative; they had time to create new things.

ANSWER KEY *(cont.)*

Day 4

1. c
2. Responses will vary but may include that no one kept records; no one enforced rules or taxes.
3. Responses will vary but should include the use of weights and measures so you know you are getting what you paid for; takes the guesswork out of buying and selling.

Day 5

1. Responses will vary but may include their religion, laws, and government.

Week 18—Civics

Day 1

1. c
2. d
3. c

Day 2

1. b
2. c
3. c

Day 3

1. c
2. Responses will vary but should include that the president is the head of the executive, legislative, and judicial branches and the army; the prime minister runs the government; laws are made, passed, and judged by different branches.
3. Responses will vary but should include that the judicial branch makes decisions when there are problems between the executive and the legislative branches.

Day 4

1. d
2. Responses will vary but should include that the Indian constitution guarantees equality, freedom of religion, education, the right to make amendments to the constitution, and the guarantee of human rights (no exploitation); our Bill of Rights guarantees these too.
3. Responses will vary but may include that it is important so that all people—regardless of race, religion, gender, or status—will receive a fair trial.

Day 5

1. Responses will vary but should include the following: United States: legislative, executive, and judicial branches; Congress can make laws and impeach government officials; it is part of the "checks and balances" system; Germany: The president has little power; the chancellor has more power; there are three branches of government: legislative, executive, and judicial; India: The president is the head of the executive, legislative, and judicial branches and the army; the prime minister runs the government; laws are made, passed, and judged by different branches.

Week 19 —Geography

Day 1

1. b
2. c
3. a

Day 2

1. a
2. c
3. b

ANSWER KEY (cont.)

Day 3
1. c
2. Responses will vary but should include North Dakota, South Dakota, Nebraska, and Kansas; states that are partially in the Great Plains include Montana, Wyoming, Colorado, New Mexico, Oklahoma, and Texas
3. Responses will vary but should include that the Rocky Mountains increase the elevation; the coastal plains are lower.

Day 4
1. b
2. b
3. Responses will vary.

Day 5
1. Responses will vary.

Week 20—Economics

Day 1
1. b
2. c
3. Responses will vary but may include the amount of government control there should be.

Day 2
1. c
2. a
3. b

Day 3
1. a, d
2. Responses will vary.
3. Responses will vary but may include that they cross state borders; they are expensive; and governments can keep fees and fares low.

Day 4
1. b
2. Responses will vary but should include that there is some government control of the economy.
3. Responses will vary but should include to the right side of the continuum, nearest "pure market economy."

Day 5
1. Responses will vary.

Week 21—History

Day 1
1. b
2. c
3. c

Day 2
1. b
2. b
3. Responses will vary but may include that each warrior would look like a different person in the afterlife.

Day 3
1. b
2. Responses will vary but could include ability to fight others.
3. So people would have to trade with them for silk.

Day 4
1. a
2. Responses will vary but may include places for guards to live; and walls with openings for weapons.
3. Responses will vary but may include the eagle, Washington Monument, the Statue of Liberty, Mount Rushmore, etc.

Day 5
1. Responses will vary but may include that in the United States today: Agriculture—is on industrial scale; Life in Cities—most of the people live in cities; Family Life—is very different; Government—democracy.

Week 22—Civics

Day 1
1. d
2. c
3. b

ANSWER KEY *(cont.)*

Day 2
1. d
2. c
3. c

Day 3
1. a
2. Responses will vary but should include that they support the Constitution; respect others, their rights, and their beliefs; volunteer; be part of the common good; obey all laws.
3. Responses will vary but may include that they can work to help others.

Day 4
1. a
2. Responses will vary but may include to gain many rights and freedoms that may not be the case in the old country.
3. Responses will vary but may include volunteering, helping those less fortunate, donating to charity, recycling, etc.

Day 5
1. Responses will vary.

Week 23—Geography

Day 1
1. b
2. b
3. b

Day 2
1. c
2. a
3. Responses will vary but should include that the Yellow River flowed around a barrier, or resistance; it followed an easy path rather than barging through a barrier; thus it changed its course, or carved a new course.

Day 3
1. a
2. b
3. Responses will vary but should include crossing desserts (extreme temperatures); plateaus/mountainous areas were challenging to climb/travel over; rivers were treacherous to cross.

Day 4
1. a
2. a
3. Responses will vary but should include that rice fields can flood with water; houses on high poles/stilts were built to avoid flooding homes; consider basements in cold climates, awnings to protect from sun's heat, windows that open to provide fresh air, etc.

Day 5
1. Responses will vary but may include that China had been closed off to the world; some of its inventions (silk), which had not been seen before, were fascinating to the world; large land mass worth exploring; in general, people are curious of the unknown.

Week 24—Economics

Day 1
1. b
2. a
3. c

Day 2
1. b
2. d
3. b

ANSWER KEY *(cont.)*

Day 3
1. c
2. Responses will vary but should include that water and the living things in the water are part of the land category.
3. Responses will vary but should include that we can run out of coal; it takes thousands of years to form; once highways are built and rainforest destroyed, the land can't easily be returned to its previous form.

Day 4
1. b
2. Responses will vary but may include not enough consumers; not earning enough profit; and too little capital to keep going.
3. Responses will vary.

Day 5
1. Responses will vary but should include reference to the land, capital (the machinery), labor (the workers), enterprise (the owner of the farm).

Week 25—History

Day 1
1. c
2. b
3. b, c, d

Day 2
1. d
2. b
3. d

Day 3
1. c
2. Responses will vary but may include strength; good fighters; good sailors.
3. Responses will vary but may include that they brought Roman traditions and laws.

Day 4
1. a
2. Responses will vary but may include school; play; chores; eating.
3. Responses will vary but may include no school for girls; the food eaten; when they went to bed.

Day 5
1. Responses will vary.

Week 26 —Civics

Day 1
1. d
2. a
3. c

Day 2
1. b
2. b
3. d

Day 3
1. c
2. c
3. Responses will vary but may include benefits such as a democratic government, education, and English being taught in schools; the United States set up a democratic government, trained teachers, and helped set up education.

Day 4
1. a
2. Responses will vary but may include as follows: Similar rights—life, liberty, property; freedom of expression (speech, press, assembly, petition, beliefs); due process, legal counsel, speedy trial; privacy; freedom of religion; vote; Similar duties—pay taxes.
3. Responses will vary but may include that Filipino schools teach patriotism, respect for human rights, respect for national heroes, rights and duties of citizens, good values, self-discipline, and thinking schools; our schools teach these, but they are not all in our Constitution.

51398—180 Days of Social Studies

ANSWER KEY *(cont.)*

Day 5

1. Responses will vary but may include the following: United States—religion; speech; press; assembly; petition; bear arms; equal justice; private property; many other freedoms; Mexico—freedom of expression (press, speech, petition, assembly); bear arms; vote or be elected; health care paid for by the government; education for all; a job and housing; freedom of religion; pay taxes; enlist in the Mexican army or the National Guard; Philippines—life, liberty, property; freedom of expression (speech, press, assembly, petition, beliefs); due process, silence, legal counsel, speedy trial; privacy; freedom of religion; travel; vote; pay taxes.

Week 27—Geography

Day 1

1. c
2. b
3. a, b

Day 2

1. c
2. c
3. a

Day 3

1. d
2. Responses will vary but may include recycling, cutting back on use, etc.
3. Responses will vary but may include, taking shorter showers, reducing lawn watering, etc.

Day 4

1. b, d
2. Responses will vary but may include water, land, electricity, machines to cut, trees.
3. Responses will vary but may include walk and don't drive; conserve water, electricity, heat, etc.

Day 5

1. Responses will vary.

Week 28—Economics

Day 1

1. d
2. c
3. c

Day 2

1. b, c
2. a, b
3. b

Day 3

1. c
2. Responses will vary but may include how they will use a scarce resource.
3. Responses will vary but may include the right-hand picture, showing conserving water.

Day 4

1. b
2. Responses will vary but may include price, flavor, and ingredients.
3. Responses will vary but may include price, flavor, and healthy food.

Day 5

1. Responses will vary but may include price, distance, and where they have visited already.

ANSWER KEY *(cont.)*

Week 29—History

Day 1
1. c
2. c
3. d

Day 2
1. b
2. a
3. c

Day 3
1. a, c
2. Responses will vary but may include need to count, record data, etc.
3. Responses will vary but may include that you can see everything in one place, at a glance; the detail makes it hard to read.

Day 4
1. c
2. Responses will vary but may include interest in ancient places; beauty of the location; etc.
3. Responses will vary.

Day 5
1. Responses will vary but may include that Moctezuma was killed by the Spanish; maybe the illness is his ghost's revenge.

Week 30—Civics

Day 1
1. c
2. c
3. d

Day 2
1. c
2. d
3. d

Day 3
1. c
2. d
3. Responses will vary but may include that his work has helped free thousands of children and open more than 100 schools; his organization trains teachers to help children with civic action.

Day 4
1. c
2. Responses will vary but should include that she has shared with the world how terrible it is to live under Taliban rule; she has helped to open many schools and educate many girls.
3. Responses will vary.

Day 5
1. Responses will vary but may include as follows: Bono: He has helped many people who were starving, poor, sick; he has petitioned governments to change laws and save people; Craig and Marc Kielburger: They have worked to end child slavery; they have opened more than 100 schools and trained teachers to help children participate in civic action; Malala Yousafzai: She let the world know about the Taliban; opened schools and helped to educate girls in a country where they have few rights.

Week 31—Geography

Day 1
1. a, b, c
2. d
3. c

Day 2
1. b
2. d
3. d

ANSWER KEY *(cont.)*

Day 3

1. a, b, c, d
2. Responses will vary but may include that people leave one region because of poor living conditions and move to another with better possibilities.
3. Responses will vary but may include that people are pushed away by poor living conditions and pulled to areas where they can have a better life.

Day 4

1. d
2. Responses will vary.
3. Responses will vary.

Day 5

1. Responses will vary but may include that people come from to the United States for freedom and a better life; they emigrate from the United States because they miss their homeland or relatives or have the possibility of work elsewhere.

Week 32—Economics

Day 1

1. c
2. b
3. b

Day 2

1. a
2. c
3. c

Day 3

1. b
2. a
3. Responses will vary but may include that the pie chart shows that manufacturing jobs declined to 7.9 percent in 2016.

Day 4

1. c
2. Responses will vary but may include that they provide a service; they don't make a physical product.
3. Responses will vary.

Day 5

1. Responses will vary but may include the following: The servers serving the food, the cook who prepared the food, the school where the food is served.

Week 33—History

Day 1

1. b
2. c
3. b

Day 2

1. c
2. c
3. c

Day 3

1. d
2. Hot temperatures because most were near the equator.
3. Responses will vary but may include communication, travel, resistance.

Day 4

1. b, c
2. Responses will vary but may include that you don't have to use beaver fur to make a good hat; are they useful hats? do they need hats?
3. Responses will vary but may include electronics from Japan or China; T-shirts and shoes from Asia; etc.

Day 5

1. Responses will vary but may include price, choice, quality, and variety.

ANSWER KEY *(cont.)*

Week 34—Civics

Day 1
1. d
2. c
3. b

Day 2
1. a
2. c
3. c

Day 3
1. c
2. Responses will vary but may include that they founded the Carter Center; it works to resolve conflicts in many countries; offer health programs; support justice and rule of law; defend human rights and equality; oversee elections; and give people information they need.
3. Responses will vary but may include that it would be important to make sure that correct rules and procedures are followed, especially in countries without democratic elections.

Day 4
1. c
2. Responses will vary but may include that she was arrested because she refused to give up her seat to a white person; this was not fair treatment; all people should be treated equally regardless of religion, gender, or race.
3. Responses will vary but may include that she showed courage and stood up for her rights during dangerous times; she helped ensure that equal rights would be given to all.

Day 5
1. Responses will vary but may include the following: Ryan White: He was a spokesperson for blood testing and HIV/AIDS treatment; Temple Grandin: She is a leader in animal rights and rights for autistic people; Rosa Parks: She was a civil rights pioneer who stood up for African Americans.

Week 35—Geography

Day 1
1. c
2. a
3. b

Day 2
1. b
2. a, b, d
3. b

Day 3
1. c
2. Responses will vary but may include more people living in an area; more traffic and congestion.
3. Responses will vary but may include land use; how communities grow; how they are managed; traffic; environment, etc.

Day 4
1. b
2. Responses will vary.
3. Responses will vary but may include safe pathways, good walking areas, safe routes through traffic, etc.

Day 5

1. Responses will vary but may include the following: Land Use: Density means more people, traffic, congestion, and pollution; Environment: pollution and health concerns in the city; Economic Trends: Development means more people moving in; more pressure on infrastructure, etc.; more taxes can mean additional public sector solutions such as public transit, etc.

Week 36—Economics

Day 1

1. c
2. b
3. c

Day 2

1. d
2. a
3. d

Day 3

1. c
2. Responses will vary but may include proximity and ease of transporting goods.
3. Responses will vary but may include not buying American goods; affects jobs; American money goes to exporters such as China; U.S. trade deficit is $347 billion.

Day 4

1. d
2. Responses will vary but may include the number of cars in the country; do not produce enough oil.
3. Responses will vary.

Day 5

1. Responses will vary but may include price and ways to improve prices; the cost of U.S. labor compared to Asia; lack of import duties and taxes.

POLITICAL MAP OF THE UNITED STATES

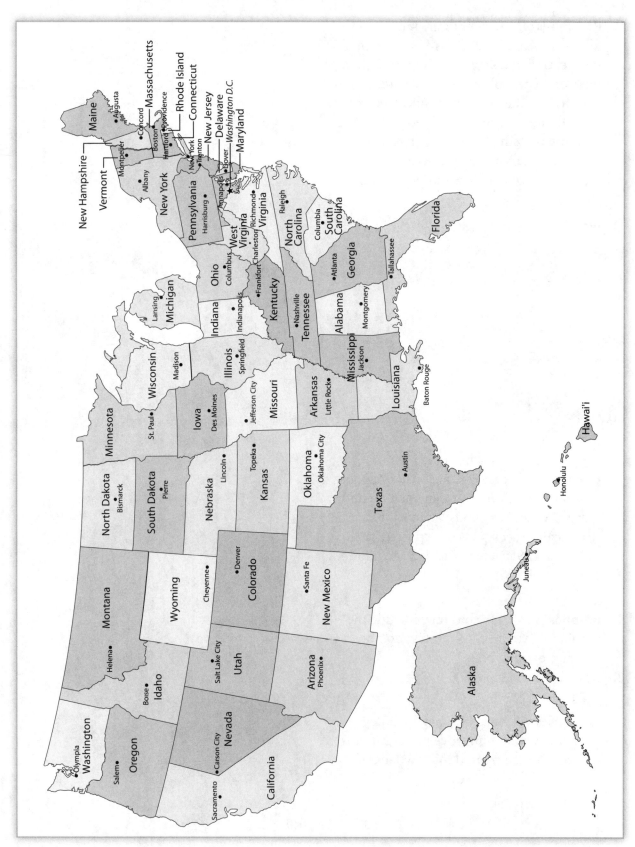

WORLD MAP

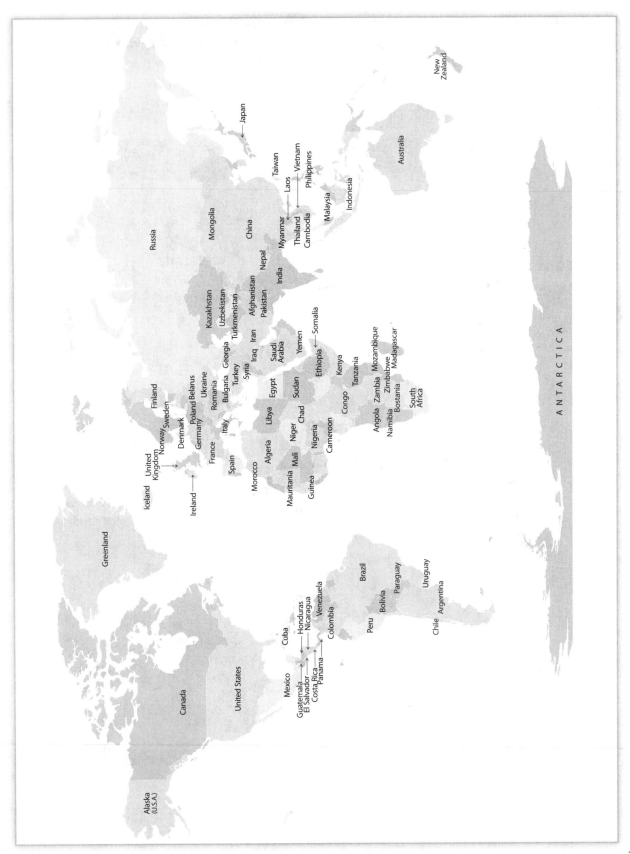

Response Rubric

Teacher Directions: The answer key provides answers for the multiple-choice and short-answer questions. This rubric can be used for any open-ended questions where student responses vary. Evaluate student work to determine how many points out of 12 students earn.

Student Name: _____

	4 Points	**3 Points**	**2 Points**	**1 Point**
Content Knowledge	Gives right answers. Answers are based on text and prior knowledge.	Gives right answers based on text.	Gives mostly right answers based on text.	Gives incorrect answers.
Analysis	Thinks about the content, and draws strong inferences/conclusions.	Thinks about the content, and draws mostly correct inferences/conclusions.	Thinks about the content, and draws somewhat correct inferences/conclusions.	Thinks about the content, and draws incorrect inferences/conclusions.
Explanation	Explains and supports answers fully.	Explains and supports answers with some evidence.	Explains and supports answers with little evidence.	Provides no support for answers.

Total: _____

51398—180 Days of Social Studies

Practice Page Item Analysis

Teacher Directions: Record how many multiple-choice questions students answered correctly. Then, record their rubric totals for Day 5. Total the four weeks of scores, and record that number in the Overall column.

Circle Week Range:	1–4	5–8	9–12	13–16	17–20	21–24	25–28	29–32	33–36		

Student Name	Day 1 Text Analysis	Day 2 Text Analysis	Day 3 Primary Source or Visual Text	Day 4 Making Connections	Day 5 Synthesis and Application	Overall
Ryan	1, 2, 2, 3	2, 2, 2, 2	2, 2, 1, 2	1, 1, 2, 1	12, 10, 12, 12	73

Student Item Analysis By Discipline

Teacher Directions: Record how many multiple-choice questions students answered correctly. Then, record their rubric totals for Day 5. Total the four weeks of scores, and record that number in the Overall column.

Student Name:

History Weeks	Day 1 Text Analysis	Day 2 Text Analysis	Day 3 Primary Source or Visual Text	Day 4 Making Connections	Day 5 Synthesis and Application	Overall
1						
5						
9						
13						
17						
21						
25						
29						
33						

Civics Weeks	Day 1 Text Analysis	Day 2 Text Analysis	Day 3 Primary Source or Visual Text	Day 4 Making Connections	Day 5 Synthesis and Application	Overall
2						
6						
10						
14						
18						
22						
26						
30						
34						

Student Item Analysis By Discipline *(cont.)*

Student Name:

Geography Weeks	**Day 1** Text Analysis	**Day 2** Text Analysis	**Day 3** Primary Source or Visual Text	**Day 4** Making Connections	**Day 5** Synthesis and Application	**Overall**
3						
7						
11						
15						
19						
23						
27						
31						
35						

Economics Weeks	**Day 1** Text Analysis	**Day 2** Text Analysis	**Day 3** Primary Source or Visual Text	**Day 4** Making Connections	**Day 5** Synthesis and Application	**Overall**
4						
8						
12						
16						
20						
24						
28						
32						
36						

Digital Resources

To access the digital resources, go to this website and enter the following code: 49701410. **www.teachercreatedmaterials.com/administrators/download-files/**.

Rubric and Analysis Sheets

Resource	Filename
Response Rubric	responserubric.pdf
Practice Page Item Analysis	itemanalysis.pdf
	itemanalysis.docx
	itemanalysis.xlsx
Student Item Analysis by Discipline	socialstudiesanalysis.pdf
	socialstudiesanalysis.docx
	socialstudiesanalysis.xlsx

Standards and Themes

Resource	Filename
Weekly Topics and Themes	topicsthemes.pdf
Standards Charts	standards.pdf